S 50

W9-DJP-669

GOSHEN COLLEGE
LIBRARY

AN INTRODUCTION TO
EDWIN ARLINGTON ROBINSON

THE MACMILLAN COMPANY
NEW YORK · BOSTON · CHICAGO · DALLAS
ATLANTA · SAN FRANCISCO

MACMILLAN & CO., Limited
LONDON · BOMBAY · CALCUTTA
MELBOURNE

**THE MACMILLAN COMPANY
OF CANADA, Limited**
TORONTO

AN INTRODUCTION TO
EDWIN ARLINGTON ROBINSON

BY

CHARLES CESTRE, A.M., D.Litt., LL.D.

PROFESSOR OF AMERICAN LITERATURE AND CIVILIZATION AT THE
UNIVERSITY OF PARIS

AUTHOR OF "THE FRENCH REVOLUTION AND ENGLISH POETS,"
"G. BERNARD SHAW AND HIS WORK," "THE IDEALS
OF FRANCE," "THE UNITED STATES"

88
BIP

New York
THE MACMILLAN COMPANY
1930

GOSHEN COLLEGE LIBRARY

811
R56c

Copyright, 1930,

By THE MACMILLAN COMPANY.

All rights reserved — no part of this
book may be reproduced in any form
without permission in writing from
the publisher.

Set up and electrotyped. Published August, 1930.

PS
3535
O2.5
Z6.2

10039
· PRINTED IN THE UNITED STATES OF AMERICA ·

The materials of this volume were first prepared for public lectures given at Bryn Mawr College in 1925. They were brought up to date and extended, the form of the original parts being preserved.

Paris, April, 1930.

CONTENTS

vii

AN INTRODUCTION TO
EDWIN ARLINGTON ROBINSON

CHAPTER I

A Modern Classic

When *The Children of the Night* made its quiet entry into the world, in 1897, lovers of poetry, who had been for years watching the horizon for a golden beam, whispered to one another that there had dawned a sign of the resurrection of Apollo on the American shore. Some hastened to cull in the little book a bunch of pretty lyrics, where gentle rhythms and musical rhymes played about simple themes. Others picked up a handful of dexterous experiments in verse, where genuine inspiration shone through delicate phrasing. A few, of more exacting taste, while enjoying the sweetness of many a *villanelle* or *ballade,* fixed their attention on terse and flexible renderings of virile thoughts, in quatrains, octaves or sonnets, cameo-poems or dramas in little, true jewels carved with exact workmanship out of solid metal. There were lines that tinkled like a silver string, couplets that sounded like a bugle-call, stanzas that rang with the full tone of an organ peal at the last period of a *rinforzando.*

The early admirers of Robinson eagerly waited for the volumes that were to follow and which did come out in unhurried succession. *Captain Craig,* a long philosophico-humorous poem, in 1902, surprised many by

1

its luxuriant growth, although most found out in it the succulent fruit that lurked under the shaggy foliage. In its protecting shade comfortably huddled such masterpieces as *Isaac and Archibald, Aunt Imogen* and *The Book of Annandale.* Then, in *The Town Down the River* (1910), the poet gave a rich crop of short compositions, ranging in matter from serene idealism to grim pleasantry, and in manner from serried compactness to mellow fluidity. 1916 saw his first great success in the judgment of a larger though still select élite, when appeared *The Man Against the Sky,* along with *Hillcrest* and *Ben Jonson Entertains a Man From Stratford.*

Merlin, his first epic drawn from the Arthurian legend, came to light the next year (1917). *Tasker Norcross,* along with *The Mill, Souvenir* and other poems, formed a volume in 1920, the same year as a second epic from the *matière de Bretagne, Lancelot. Avon's Harvest* together with *Rembrandt to Rembrandt* went into print in 1921. Then followed a novel in verse *Roman Bartholow* (1923), a dramatic narrative, *The Man Who Died Twice* (1924), the satirical sketch *Dionysus in Doubt* (1925), with a fine collection of *Sonnets.*

The third great epic, *Tristram* (1927), which was to complete the Arthurian trilogy, so majestically and movingly interpreted the world-famous mediaeval romance that the outstanding excellences of Robinson's verse, thus far ignored by the larger public, forced themselves into recognition, and he, after thirty years' patient waiting and unflagging trust in his own genius, at last was greeted with universal applause. Although Amer-

ica, in the interval, had witnessed an exceptional efflor-
escence of good poetry, he was hailed not only as the
dean, but as the prince of American bards.

Those who have made the personal acquaintance of
Robinson know that poetical genius with him does not
preclude perfect equipoise of thought. Glory is not
likely to have flushed him with undue elation or to have
materially altered his deliberate attitude towards life
and art. Whatever legitimate gratification he may
have felt at seeing the cultivated American readers won
over to him *en masse,* there must have lingered in his
mind a streak of gentle irony concerning the casualness
of public opinion in matters intellectual. He is too
courteous and humane to minimize the significance of
a nation-wide current of popular favor, however belated.
But his cool and composed judgment had long pondered
on the destiny of works of art. How many are there
who prize a poet to his full worth, while he stands in
the crowd, uttering words that seem cheap as long as
they can be expected to flow on from day to day? Is it
Rembrandt alone who said to himself:

> What if in fifty or a hundred years
> They find you out?

The bulk and quality of Robinson's production during thirty years testify that he found sufficient countenance and support in the joy of work and in the strength
of his creative power. Niggard or lavish, public praise
seems to him a luxury. He never lacked the spur of his
own genius nor the backing of the choice few: that was

3

enough. Did he not say (more truly of himself than of any other member of the guild):

> As long as Fame's imperious music rings
> Will poets mock it with crowned words august.

He never stooped to humor vulgar tastes by whittling off pretty figurines, polishing smooth intaglios or hammering away fearful "engines" of terror. His manner has always been that of the inspired reader of life, the attentive observer of character, the searching explorer of the secret conflicts of the heart. There are ample proofs in his work of his being able, if he had so chosen, to court easy success by feats of virtuosity. But his call was to play the sympathetic witness to human joys and sorrows. He never sacrificed the higher interests of art to any clever trick of legerdemain or the facile performance of side-shows. What he felt to be the best way to convey truth touched to beauty—by solid strokes of meaning welded to subtle shades of expression—has always had his exclusive preference. Images and metaphors, sprung from a vivid vision and a rare sense of wonder, naturally mingle with the stream of experience and reflection. Impassioned utterance throbs at moments of heightened emotion. Color and pathos intervene, subordinated to the exact dosage of the ingredients of thought.

Robinson never swerved from the interpretation of life and the conception of art which he had adopted at the outset after facing the problems on which rest conduct, happiness and faith. He cheerfully accepted poverty—the noble, simple mode of existence which suits contemplation and the toil of creation—rather than neglect his proper task of delineating true visages and painting the order or disorder of man's world with entire probity. His firmness of purpose, his allegiance to truth, his trust in destiny, his glad acceptance of hardship, compose a handsome and dignified life-pattern matched by his poetic achievement. Both bear the mark of the classic spirit.

Robinson, as poet, deserves to be styled a modern classic, because he combines in harmonious union the old-time qualities of intellectual acumen, broad humanity, universal appeal, decorum, sense of proportion and art of composition, with powers more recently developed as means of literary expression: imaginative coloring, sensuous richness, suggestive foreshortenings and word melody. A survey of his work yields the impression of wealth of vision and felicity of technique, together with a concern for what is most human in man: preference for the general, subordination of sensation to sensibility and of sensationalism to sense, propriety and reserve—all which remind us of ancient Greece and Rome, and of the Augustan age in France and in England. His occasional adaptations and variations of Greek themes fit in so exactly with his own work that they seem to be a spontaneous retrospect of his thought towards the past. His most original creations, with all their keen analysis of the moods and idiosyncrasies of our time, bear the unmistakable stamp of the per-

5

manently human. The personal, modern and American flavor of his observation inserts itself with the most natural suitableness into a reading of life and character that will last for ages.

Owing to his sure sense of moral sanity and artistic restraint, Robinson has been able to avoid the eccentricities into which a morbid craving for excitement and a frivolous disregard of mental balance and delicacy has often inveigled the writers of the present day. He has kept himself free from the hectic pruriency that seems to have overpowered for a time literary modesty and the traditional reluctance of the public to the unguarded expression of fleshly appetites. No lure of spurious success could make him believe that a complacency for the grosser manifestations of the sex-instinct was a valuable conquest in the field of esthetics or a fair adjunct to artistic enjoyment. Yet there has been no squeamishness on his part. He has too thoroughly appropriated what there is of value in the new psychology not to grant to the physical its legitimate claim as the necessary substratum of the psychical. And he is too open-minded a student of social facts to ignore the unpleasant aspects of human behavior.

But unpleasantness may be glossed over so as to palliate apparent deformity. Robinson raises realism to the plane of the imaginative, brightening drab features by comely metaphors.

> You are what it is that over rose-blown gardens
> Makes a pretty flutter for a season in the sun,

6

You are what it is that with a mouse, Jane Wayland,
Catches him and lets him go and eats him up for fun.

Or he takes advantage of a scriptural phrase to cover
the offensiveness of sin:

> . . . our talk renewed the tinge
> Of a long-faded scarlet fringe.

John Evereldown is no saint; Fernando Nash no con-
scientious objector to strong drinks; yet there does not
occur one harsh-sounding word in the stories that tell
of their pitiable ordeal. No unwholesomeness, under
color of ingenuous confidence or scientific accuracy.
No crudity, under color of social investigation. No loudness, under color of echoing the din of modern cities,
from factory whistles to automobile honks or students'
yells.

Excess of any sort is banished from Robinson's poetry. He shows himself as averse to angelic goodness
as to devilish villainy. The glaring contrasts, affected
by the seekers after sensation, he sets aside as distor-
tions of human nature fit to shock the nerves rather
than stir the emotions. His characters are distinguished by a balance of qualities and defects, tempered
by a fine play of lights and shadows. A Craig, a Flammonde, the derelict of *Old Trails* are failures in whom
there lives some redeeming grace, whether an inborn
buoyancy of heart that keeps them in tune with the beat
of the universe, or an engaging address, or a gift of human sympathy that makes them teachers of kindness, or

7

a smouldering fire that blazes up opportunely to illumine the darkness where they were sinking. Bewick Finzer, the unfortunate speculator on 'Change, preserves in his decadence a dignity which gains him the esteem and ready help of others. Even Bokardo, too far gone to muster strength and put up a fight with fate, is not without a friend who sees in him some promise of resiliency.

Character-painting has always attracted classic writers in prose or in verse, from Theophrastus to La Bruyère and the wits of Queen Anne's time. Robinson, after Browning, introduces into this *genre* the novelty of presenting his originals through a monologue, delivered by the man himself or addressed to him by a familiar. It takes away the stiffness of formal narrative. It introduces the physical incidents and mental features indirectly, through the fits and starts of living speech, by intimation and suggestion, according to the natural emergence of ideas and the spontaneous flow of feelings. The inner physiognomy of the personages gradually looms up through a luminous dazzle of little color-dots, thought-splashes and dramatic hints. The reader is called on to collaborate, by reconstructing the picture in his mind. The effect is startling. If we miss the gist of it at the first reading, a little more concentrated attention will bring out the lineaments of the portrait with all their vividness. We do not grudge our pains, since a moderate amount of pleasurable intellectual exertion will yield far more than the cursory perusal of more obvious and less significant material.

The method, modern as it is, derives from the classic

tradition, for, under the surface-impressions, there lies
in the author's mind a clean-cut structure, impalpable
but as firmly drawn as a Raphael cartoon, the logic of
which directs the apparently free outward development
and gathers the details into a well-knit whole. The
key-stone of the fabric, in the longer poems, is often an
inner dramatic conflict, based on the struggle between
reason and passion.

In the poem which opens the series, *The Book of Annandale,* love is at grips with deliberate thought within
the breast of the two characters, Annandale and Damaris. In the case of either, reason leagued with sorrow is assaulted by growing passion. The man and the
woman do not seek each other; they are irresistibly
urged by a subconscious force. Both the widower and
the widow are independently debating with themselves,
in order to settle whether they shall remain faithful to
the memory of their dead partner, or whether they
shall listen to the voice from the depths and respond
to the call of life. The antagonistic motives in them
are unequally strong, but vigorous enough to keep
their own ground in a protracted battle. Passion leashed
in by reason gradually drags reason along, yet influ-
enced by the moderator—a classic theme of balance and
restraint, beautifully treated by the poet, who can both
side with the strength of the rational check and give
his sympathy to the yearnings of the heart. Pent up
love at the end bursts out in a lyrical flow, the more
moving as it was longer repressed. Idealism lifts up
its song, without any romantic bluster.

In *Merlin* and in *Lancelot,* the dramatic motive is a

love-parting inevitably brought about by fateful circumstances. The externals of the situation, in the two narratives, bear some resemblance. The genius of the poet has succeeded in giving to each a striking individuality. The magic lies in the keen intellectual discrimination between the characters. Merlin is too well seasoned in the ways of courts to be capable of wholly ingenuous love. There lurks in Vivian too much of half-unconscious artfulness for her to give her soul up in unqualified heart-surrender. Out of curiosity and a temporary need of imaginative excitement, the two engage in a love-adventure where they half fancy themselves in earnest and half realize the highly sophisticated nature of the *liaison*. They move in an atmosphere of esthetic make-believe. Their appearance, their speech, their gestures, the *décor* that surrounds them are exquisitely theatrical. They play a "mask of love," to an accompaniment of hautboys, flutes and viols, in dresses of purple and gold, under green arbors, by the side of fountains where red fishes flash scarlet gleams. A sweet reasonableness hovers over their graceful abandon; for Merlin, being wise beyond ordinary human foresight, knows the love of the admiring young princess for his august person cannot last for ever; and Vivian, wrapt as she is in conscious wonder, has a brooding suspicion that the king-maker will some day hear the haunting call from beyond the sea. They part in sadness, with a melancholy conviction that human happiness is a fragile possession; but there is no gnashing of teeth, no outcry of despair.

10

Lancelot as fiery in his mistress' bower as on the battlefield—Guinevere, born with unfathomed depths of passion in her heart—do we not feel that only compelling forces, inside and outside them, can wrench them from each other's arms? When the sky lours over them, the Queen clings to her paramour with the desperate tenacity of one who feels that, if she lose him, she gives away all reason to live. Lancelot thinks and thinks, vainly trying to ward off the thought that, if they stay together, it will be the ruin of both. The poet, with his classic grasp of the essence of tragedy, chose for the central scene the anguished moment when Fate is about to close his claw on the two lovers. Fate is the embodiment of their wild passion. Guinevere's frantic attempt to retain Lancelot, were it by flight with him to France where she would accept to hide in a peasant's cottage for the rest of her days, reaches the climax of pathetic appeal. Lancelot's complex state of mind exemplifies the struggle for rational self-possession on the part of a man caught in a storm of frightful inner disturbance. He is still the passionate lover; but his chivalrous spirit, his loyalty to his liege-lord and to his fellow-knights do not allow him to give up honor and to sacrifice so many precious lives to the tyranny of love. The Light that he saw gleaming afar, where Galahad had found the Grail, fortifies his attachment to the moral ideal. Above all, he cannot brook that Guinevere should be doomed, even at her request, to wander in exile, fallen from her eminence and splendor. Better for her to accept Arthur's pardon, and for him to depart—alone with his grief. The pathos of the scene arises from the heart-torture which cool reason and moral scruple inflict on a man who had placed his idealism in love and who realizes that this splendid illusion cannot resist the encounter with higher and more permanent ideals.

In the third Arthurian epic, the *Tristram,* Robinson has struck the topmark of beauty and pathos. The exceptional merit of the poem is due to the wistful thoughtfulness of the characters in the grasp of an irresistible passion, to the decorous intensity of the feelings, to the perfect art of composition and the subdued glow of the style—in a word, to the classic artistry which decks the old romantic tale with proportionate and equable beauty. The theme is divested from the meretricious ornaments which in the mediaeval version somewhat blur its intrinsic directness. Character-painting, dialogue, lyrical outflow, dramatic impact are focused on the one central purpose: the vivid, harmonious, moving presentation of the most enthralling love-story in the world, re-told with all its fascinating glamour, yet kept free from excess by an admirable poise of thought, faultless taste in the management of the emotions, and an effective handling of Fate as an awful reminder of the transience of human happiness. Robinson's art seems to have taken its inspiration from the easeful majesty of Greek sculpture and the deep earnestness of the paintings of Leonardo. Antique sense of form and modern sense of strength are fused in such exact proportion that the ultimate result is a perfect work of

art, fit to soothe and exalt, "of linkèd sweetness long
drawn out."

The heroes of the Arthurian epics are exceptional beings enmeshed in such inextricable entanglements of
passion and circumstance that they are doomed to a
tragic destiny. Their reason and will keep them afloat
for a time, giving them a chance "to strut and fret an
hour" on the stage of this world, and, when ruin or death
overpowers them, to foresee the end and know why
they fall or die. Therein is contained the catharsis by
which the Greeks raised tragedy to a higher level than
madness or bloodshed, and made it a lesson of moral
steadfastness or noble resignation.

In the shorter poems, Robinson generally eschews
the extremity of utter defeat or hopeless desperation.
His aim is to rouse our thoughtful sympathy. He does
it by describing the gusts of passion or the throes of
consciousness in his characters, but stops short of any
violent catastrophe. The inner drama overrules the
outer drama. The passions are not allowed to become
unmanageable or to run amuck. The intellect plays a
notable part; the head keeps its ground under the assaults of the heart. The characters—who are often
the narrators of their own stories—are presented at moments when they are able to retrace their emotions with
some degree of composure.

Let us examine, in some of the poems, how that inter-
action of thought and feeling is effected.

The Clinging Vine: A jilted wife, in the midst of her

13

anger against her fickle husband, finds some sort of comfort in the thought that the other woman will soon have to go through the same experience.

Eros Turannos: An ill-mated woman, full of resentment for the missed happiness, reflects that it will be a lesser evil for her to nurse the feeble gleam of affection she still feels, than moodily to break off the marriage tie.

Partnership: The saving ray capable of dispelling the mist that darkens two lives, may be long to come; but even if it dawns on a death-bed, it is not too late.

London Bridge: There is a period in a woman's life when, if her nerves are not steady, wild imaginations will rush into her mind, with such power of impact that her life and that of her husband and children may be shattered,—unless her husband keeps cool and, with mixed argument and authority, brings her back to her senses.

In such poems, Robinson stands at variance with what has been called the "insurgent" movement in contemporary American literature. If we readers of the XXth century lent ourselves unreservedly to the influence of a number of writings that claim to mirror the modern spirit, we might cease to believe that the greatness of man is to be a rational being. A large part of the literature of to-day seems to have become a free field for impulse to ramp in, with sensation and sensuality as companions. Reason and conscience undergo an eclipse. Were we to take much of the printed account of our time for actual truth, we might think we are living in

14

a pandemonium of mad appetite and crazy fantasy. Robinson never yielded to the temptation of joining the wild dance. He raised no protest. An inborn aversion to the didactic turns him away from moralizing. Occasionally a thrust of sharp irony hits some contemporary ridicule. But he prefers avoiding the particular and ephemeral, to deal with the larger aspects of life. Whatever he touches, his way is that of the creative artist. He makes men and women talk, act, live, before us and, through a skillful handling of their behavior and speech, he intimates his own interpretation of character and conduct. Even if his personages make a mess of their lives, they suggest by contrast facts of the mind and soul-values that pertain to our higher nature and raise us above the mean and commonplace. It is that implied moral, closely connected with intellectual analysis and a firm grasp of experience, which gives Robinson's verse a quality that we feel entitled to call classic.

The Growth of Lorraine introduces an unpleasant subject, treated with delicacy and human commiseration, and such sure management of immanent justice that the material contained in a pair of sonnets bulks as large as a two-act drama. Two phases of a fast girl's life: the gay one, bold, cynical, defiant; the dark one, spasmodic, dejected, pitiful, with a dash of the old daring to meet death deliberately. It is marvellous that so much terror, pity and truth can be enclosed in so little space—and expressed so poignantly. Realism, thus distinguished by sobriety, dignity and elevation, is a new literary force, a splendid creation.

15

The resourcefulness of the poet appears in the ease with which he tackles a great variety of subjects and makes use of widely dissimilar metrical forms. His fullness of thought and richness of sentiment are strikingly original in *The Wilderness,* a dramatic lyric which tells, in musical stanzas, linked by a refrain, the disappointment of west-bound pioneers, stopped by early snow in the Rocky Mountains. They reluctantly give up their dream of triumphant adventure; but the vision of the home-coming, the anticipation of the unexpected meeting with the dear ones who stayed behind, assuage their grief. A gorgeous description of autumn on the Great Divide, plaintive regrets and longings lyrically chanted, bold strokes of thought reaching out to the Unknown, make the poem ring like a magnificent anthem. Robinson's classic qualities—his intellectual awareness, his grasp of the general through the particular, his respect for the truths of the conscience and of the heart—harmonize naturally with the grand lyrical inspiration.

His lyricism is tinged with melancholy, because he sees with a realist's eye the mixed nature of human joys and the precarious standing of human happiness. In the light of this wisdom every character or situation appears with its bright and its dark side. There are neither spotless individuals nor unblemished favors of destiny. The poet steers clear of ecstatic dreams and of gross disillusions. His greatness dwells in mild pathos associated with conscious serenity. The attractiveness of the characters lies in a striving after

16

mental and moral balance, which, even if unsuccessful, wears the nobleness of worthy intention and endeavor. To this view of life can be ascribed some of his best reflective sonnets and most touching narratives.

The married couple, in *Firelight,* who silently bask in mutual trust, would not be so happy, did not both the man and the woman repress the memory of an older and stronger love. Two friends, in *The Long Race,* who are going to meet again after many years, eagerly anticipate the joy of recalling the bright hopes of bygone times; when they do stand in presence of each other they are only able to talk trifles; they part crushed under the weight of the sad inhibition.

How easily we deceive ourselves, not only when we try to retain dreams of present happiness, but when we foster in our hearts promises of everlasting reward! Only a few realize how steep is the way that leads to the summits,

> . . . and for cause not always plain,
> They are the laggards among those who strive
> On earth to raise the golden dust of heaven. (*The Laggards*)

Where can we find more likeable old men than Isaac and Archibald? We love bustling, eager Isaac, trotting along a sandy road in the scorching midsummer sun, as he goes to see what his friend is to do with his oats. We love hearty, patient Archibald, sitting in the shade of his orchard and talking of the plenty that will reward his year of toil. We are fond of both good-natured patriarchs, with their pastoral mellowness and

17

their partiality for a goblet of cider and a game of seven-up. Why should we not indulgently smile when each of them in his turn tells in confidence the boy-companion, who enjoys their hospitality, that he notices signs of decline in his friend? Are they not the more true to common mortality for that readiness to detect in the other what they are blind to in themselves?

Equally worthy of all esteem and affection is Aunt Imogen, so devotedly attached to her sister's children, in spite of the bitter jealousy that she feels at times gnawing at her heart under stress of the overpowering thought of her loneliness. We sympathize with her pain and admire the pluck with which she keeps a bright face and lets no one suspect the agonizing qualm.

Pathos is there tempered by kind-heartedness and self-control. That the poet, when he chooses, can sound the depths of soul-torture or fateful despair is testified by the tragic intensity of some great scenes in the Arthurian epics or in dark tales like *Tasker Norcross, Avon's Harvest* and *Roman Bartholow*.

In contrast, the "spirit of comedy," as defined by Meredith, manifests itself in the poet's irony, which peers through the infirmities, follies or deficiencies of man's nature, not of enough importance to cause ruin or death but sufficient to deprive life of its fruition of reasonableness or beauty. Satire has always been the gift of the attentive observers of social behavior. It is an element of the classic genius. Robinson, a clear-eyed realist and prober of psychological facts, possesses it to a high degree. He does not generally resort to incisive banter. To front-attacks he prefers the indirect, insinuating pricks of humorous suggestion. When he does occasionally turn to open stricture, it is under the urge of some strong provocation. Thus his Cassandra hurls biting censure at the materialism of contemporary America.

> Your Dollar is your only Word,
> The wrath of it your only fear. . . .
> Are you to pay for what you have
> With all you are?

The smug complacency of party politicians does not blind him to the shallowness of their professions:

> A fevered glimpse of a democracy
> Confused and foiled with an equality
> Not equal to the envy it creates.

Let Americans open their minds to the lesson of history and to the truths of human nature:

> See not the great among you for the small,
> But hear their silence; for the few shall save
> The many, or the many are to fall—
> Still to be wrangling in a noisy grave.

Those are unpleasant warnings to citizens spoiled with prosperity, overflowing with optimism and cheerfully indifferent to their errors as long as plenty, comfort and good humor deck the road to brave achievement. It is not only his own compatriots that Robinson feels impelled to sting with burning words, in the hope of goading them to reform. Humanity at large he can "use after its desert." *The Valley of the Shadow* draws a sombre but needful picture of the absurd way in which men let themselves sink in despair or settle in despondency. Why should they pursue idle fancies that never had any connection with reality?

> There were pensioners of dreams and there were debtors of
> illusions,
> All to fail before the triumph of a weed that only grows.

Why should they exult in the pride of what they deem exceptional gifts,—which are only pitiful eccentricities?

> There were blighted sons of wonder in the Valley of the
> Shadow,
> Where they suffered and still wondered why their wonder
> made no noise.

Why do they not know how to extract from life the balm which it can distil as well as the bitterness?

> And there were daughters older than the mothers who had
> borne them,
> Being older in their wisdom, which is older than the earth.

Why can they not learn necessary resignation?

> And over beauty's aftermath of hazardous ambitions
> There were tears for what had vanished as they vanished
> where they fell.

Alas! Those who are least unhappy are the unfortunates stunned by grief and disappointment:

There were seekers after darkness in the Valley of the
    Shadow,
And they alone were there to find what they were looking for.

Usually the smart of the irony is softened by a salve
of soothing words. How gently we are made acquainted
with the case of Briony, the millionaire, who with heaps
of untold gold at his beck and call, lives in daily anguish:

> Others are flourishing worse than he,
> But he knew too much for the life he led.

Look at the portrait of the lady "cursed with happiness,"
in *Captain Craig*. She is a busy-body, an unconscious
dissembler, with a vacuum in her brains and a clod in
the place of a heart. All this is decorously embedded
in a beautiful image:

>   . . . and there she goes,
> Like a whirlwind through an orchard in the springtime —
> Throwing herself away as if the world
> Were a flourish of apple-blossoms.

Job the Rejected had been waiting patiently until the
woman he loved found out that her husband was a hol-
low sham. Expectant, he began to entertain hopes:

> But Job was not, so far as we could say,
> The confirmation of her soul's desire.

No smooth periphrasis or glowing metaphor, on the
other hand, can suit the poet's purpose when the cause

of his displeasure calls less for irony than for indignation. He will then brook no sleek words to interfere between his anger and the reproof. Thus, in *The Man Against the Sky,* he mercilessly exposes the disgrace of the unprincipled recanter:

> And at his heart there may have gnawed
> Sick memories of a dead faith foiled and flawed
> And long dishonored by the living death
> Assigned alike by chance
> To brutes and hierophants.

Just severity bespeaks no hardness of heart. It is rather the sure sign of a sensibility ready to respond, when called on, to the stimulus of all gentle feelings. What depth of tenderness in the poems dedicated to dear persons! They are not love poems; for classic restraint is too strong with Robinson to allow him ever to depart from the strict principle of objectivity. He wrote exquisite verse for a little girl of five, Arvia, whose large eyes, raised in wonder, were like the lamps of her soul. And he mourned the death of a beautiful young woman in accents that deserve to be placed side by side with the most moving threnodies. The two poems bear the hallmark of his genius by the manner in which they associate with the feelings of admiration and regret, far-reaching vistas opening on boundless horizons.

Robinson's poetry, at its highest, overleaps the barriers of realism and expands in the sphere of liberated thought, where reason and faith, transcending the accidents of mortal life, descry the beauty and hopefulness of ultimate values.   In his early compositions, he expressed the creed of a Christian liberal with a fervor and breadth of view, that, disregarding orthodoxy, went straight to the pure teaching of Jesus.   Later, he voiced his faith in the spiritual without reference to any formal belief, laying trust in his conscience, in the undying hope of man, and in the promise that never fails the prophetic heart.   Has he no doubts?   Far from shutting his eyes to the tokens that warn us of the obstacles on the way, far from ignoring the uncertainty there is for any of us to achieve the ideal, he weighs all the evidence, and, like Montaigne, uses the keen light of his intellect to clear a little patch of his own in this vast entangled world.   He hesitates—not so much with regard to the problem of individual betterment, as concerning the future of human communities.   He says in *The Garden of the Nations:*

> And when we are all gone, shall mightier seeds
> And scions of a warmer spring put forth
> A bloom and fruitage of a larger worth
> Than ours?   God save the garden, if by chance,
> Or by approved short sight, more numerous weeds
> And weevils be the next inheritance!

Merlin, who speaks for individual man with the large wisdom of a seer, ordained to instruct his fellow-creatures in a more rational behavior and a better use of their opportunities, although he measures the length and severity of the ordeal, keeps a firm faith in the destiny of mankind:

Or there may be still charted for his feet
A dimmer faring, where the touch of time
Were like the passing of a twilight moth
From flower to flower into oblivion,
If there were not somewhere a barren end
Of moths and flowers, and glimmering far away,
Beyond a desert where the flowerless days
Are told in slow defeats and agonies,
The guiding of a nameless light. . . .

Robinson's teaching may be summed up in Emerson's words: "Man is a golden impossibility."

A great poet can create lasting beauty and do his proper task of torch-bearer to the generations only if his form adds the final touch of outward excellence to the inner qualities. Robinson is assured to have his place in the Hall of Fame, because of the perfect correspondence in his work of the manner to the matter.

The student of his poetical style must distinguish between his stripped language—used for realistic description, narration or dialogue, and for character-painting or psychological analysis, whenever fact or thought predominates over feeling—and his sumptuous language, which nobly swells to a high degree of imaginative coloring, impassioned intensity and rhythmical amplitude under the breath of inspiration, as the ocean surges into mighty waves when the hurricane wields it to its will.

Stripped does not mean tame or bare. Robinson's style in its simpler garb has the qualities of aptness, precision and sobriety, and offers a nicety of structure and a fullness of meaning, which are generally associated with classical economy of words and compactness of design. Striking effects are produced by the mere pertinency of terms, used with their whole expressiveness and set in the exact place, like diamonds in a tiara. How felicitously some lines sound to the mind and to the ear! For instance, in *Flammonde,* the advice given by the poet to the Puritans:

> Nor need we nourish an ethical unrest . . .

in *The Gift of God,* the expression of the infatuated mother's admiration for her son:

> The firm fruition of her need,
> He shines anointed . . .

in *Old Trails,* the humorous traits:

> Behold a ruin who meant well . . .
> I haven't failed; I've merely not achieved . . .
> Though you are silent, what you say is true . . .
> My dreams have all come true to other men . . .
> They chill drinks here with ice from hell. . . .

in *The Unforgiven,* the acid anger of the ageing wife:

> And she, the unforgiving, hates him
> More for her lack than for her loss.

in *Bewick Finzer,* the sad decay of a once prosperous financier:

> The broken voice, the withered neck,
>   The coat worn out with care,
> The cleanliness of indigence,
>   The brilliance of despair,
> The fond imponderable dreams
>   Of affluence,—all were there.

In the last quotation, the fitness of the rhythm to the sense and the ship-shape cut of the stanza help to carry over the meaning and add beauty to thought. There is a great variety of metrical measures and of stanza-forms in Robinson's work, and each is planned to introduce the exact musical accompaniment to the intellectual content. It is to be noted that, among other devices, he revived the traditional couplet, with variations of his own, linking the two lines less by the final rhyme than by the sense and the beat, and using them to bring out a striking parallelism or contrast in the thought. The spare use he makes of this prosodic feature makes it the more effective. Thus, in *Her Eyes:*

> With a gleam of heaven to make them pure,
> And a glimmer of hell to make them human.

In *The Unforgiven*, the woman is possessed of a tyrannical witchery:

> To blind a man till he be glad,
> And humble him till he be mad.

in *The Woman and the Wife:*

> The dark is at the end of every day,
> And silence is the end of every song.

26

in *Flammonde:*

> His mien distinguished any crowd,
> His credit strengthened when he bowed.

Words full of meaning and of suggestion, that convey a plenitude of thought and bear a rareness of aristocratic and esthetic grace, lines and stanzas that express in outward fluidity and order the inner strength and harmony, are splendid materials for composition. In his architectonics, Robinson often combines the logic of ideas with a natural flow of the feelings and an effective conduct of the dramatic interest, with unwonted success.

This is not quite the case with the *Lancelot,* where some parts do not reach the highest pitch. It is but a comparative lack, in comparison with the other Arthurian epics; we mention it because the sustained beauty of the other poems makes us fastidious. A few scenes—King Arthur's wrath, the parting of the lovers at Joyous Gard and their farewell at Almesbury—are powerfully treated; but the rest of the poem seems rather artificial, made up of incidents and dialogues of secondary interest. The *Merlin* and the *Tristram,* on the other hand, rise, swell and fall with the magnificent sweep of an equinoctial tide.

In *The Man Who Died Twice,* we find the same masterly structure, whereas *Roman Bartholow* somewhat halts in the middle and lags at the end. What great poet was always equal to himself? The defect to which Robinson is exposed by the very fineness of his intellectuality is to let oversubtle analysis interfere with the directness of the narrative or the rapidity of the dramatic development. He is apt to lapse into undue lengthiness or obscurity. We cannot say that *Tasker Norcross* and *Avon's Harvest* are absolutely free from such blemishes. But *Ben Jonson Entertains a Man From Stratford* can hardly be found fault with, while the incisive characterization, the literary insight, the dignified humor, the imaginative flights, the elevation of thought make the poem a noble and inspiring rendering of one of the greatest subjects that could be treated.

In the shorter pieces, there may be occasionally—when elaborate thought gets the better of spontaneous inspiration—a certain stiffness or awkwardness. More often the happy alliance of firm conception with lofty feeling and perfect composition can produce such a thing of beauty as *Exit*. In three stanzas of four lines is presented a pathetic plea for a man who, once the cynosure of all eyes, was found wanting and fell from his eminence, wounded to death by the blow, yet stoical to the end, taking refuge in proud silence. The poem is like one of those miniature triptychs that adorn old chapel-altars. Three panels, each with a similar grouping of motives and a similar scheme of colors, each expressing the same general feeling, each bringing its contribution by a shade of thought or a touch of emotion, each engraving on our minds lines whose sum-total produces the moving final effect. For its terseness, its restrained pathos, its musical sweetness and its shapely outline, it is one of the best examples of Robinson's art of composition and classic sense of decorum and proportion. The piece is so short that it can be quoted entire:

> For what we owe to other days,
> Before we poisoned him with praise,
> May we who shrank to find him weak
> Remember that he cannot speak.
>
> For envy that we may recall,
> And for our faith before the fall,
> May we who are alive be slow
> To tell what we shall never know.
>
> For penance he would not confess,
> And for the fateful emptiness
> Of early triumph undermined,
> May we now venture to be kind.

This feat of intellectual neatness and emotional concentration was repeated more than once by the poet, especially in the sonnets. Robinson is a master of the sonnet. He adopts the most difficult form: two quatrains followed by two tercets. In the middle there is a pause, which divides the thought into two parts, the latter being the antithesis, or the complement, or the conclusion to the former. Not only does the poet observe the rules with ease, but he marshals the complex rhyme-scheme with brilliancy, almost without resorting to run-on lines that break the rhythm and mar the sense. His sonnets continue the great tradition of English literature, with obeisance to none.

There remains to mention an element of poetical achievement, seldom to be found in natural association with the classical bent of mind, but which forms a genuine and important part of Robinson's equipment— namely the imagination. It accounts for some of the poet's most powerful creations. The study of allegory and symbol, of the suggestion of mystery and infinity, is reserved for another chapter. I wish to point out here how often, in individual lines or in short poems, the imagination enhances the thought and gives it a magic sway over the reader's mind. An imaginative touch is sometimes contained in a single word or line, or in a brief poetical period. Thus, Shakespeare urged by his haunting desire to own an estate at Stratford is described as

> manor-bitten to the bone.

Captain Craig, the lover of sunshine, listens ecstatically to

> the gold-throated forward call.

In *For a Dead Lady,* how weirdly touching is the plaint:

> No more shall quiver down the days
> The flowing wonder of her ways.

Merlin, alone, spell-bound by the image in his brain of Vivian's bewitching attractiveness,

> felt the picture of her beauty
> And shivered at the nearness of her being.

30

In *The Voice of Age,* what strange, faded gracefulness is
contained in the description:

> Her mystical serene address
> Of age alloyed with loveliness.

In *Veteran Sirens,* how decorous and sympathetic the
attitude of the poet in presence of shattered lives and
ruined beauty:

> The burning hope, the worn expectancy,
> The martyred humor, and the maimed allure,
> Cry out for time to end his levity,
> And age to soften its investiture.

Imaginative snatches are often introduced in connection with the beauty of nature. Natural description is seldom treated by Robinson with deliberate purpose and for its own sake. When it does intervene, it
comes in like a ray of sunshine filtering through foliage.
Who does not remember the cherry-blossoms falling on
the garden-path at Broceliande? and Vivian's green
arbor by the fountain? Who has not felt the beauty of
the bright flash of the oak-leaves above Guinevere's
golden hair? Who but was entranced by the magnificent sunset scene in the second part of *Tristram?* Let
me recall here the less known poem, *Archibald's Example,* where the old man explains so movingly why he
caused the cluster of fir-trees at the top of the hill to
be cut down:

> My green hill yonder, where the sun goes down
> Without a scratch, was once inhabited
> By trees that injured him—an evil trash
> That made a cage, and held him while he bled.

31

The simplest words, selected from every-day speech, suffice to express in a thrilling, realistic evocation, the communion with nature which oriental prophets have embodied in sacred myths. Robinson does not call himself an imagist, but he can conjure pictures often more vivid to the mind's eye than those of the professed imagists.

The passage just quoted belongs to the stripped manner, here applied to a universal feeling shared in alike by poets and by farmers. In order to illustrate Robinson's wide range of imagination and the ease with which he passes from the familiar to the sublime, here is, in contrast, a poem of eight lines, *The Dark Hills,* where thought, image and mystical vision unite, at the bidding of a powerful emotion, and call to their service lofty language in sumptuous array. It is an after-war piece. The poet stands in sight of a row of hills, fronting the west, where men fought and were buried. It is sunset time. The splendor of the sky seems to sound a flourish in honor of the dead. They sleep. With the passing of the last afterglow, the earth also goes to sleep. Is it the hour of rest for the world, and the end of wars?

> Dark hills at evening in the west,
> Where sunset hovers like a sound
> Of golden horns that sang to rest
> Old bones of warriors under ground,
> Far now from all the bannered ways
> Where flash the legions of the sun,
> You fade—as if the last of days
> Were fading, and all wars were done.

I shall have to quote several passages, of equal splendor when I comment on the bulk of the work in more detail and from various points of view. In the best poems, the same pregnant union will be found of a firmly conceived subject, drawn from the agile observation of the ways of the world or the penetrating reading of the depths of the heart, with a mode of expression which, simple or magnificent, successfully effects the transposition from the abstract to the concrete, and illustrates thought with image, as only great poets have done, since poetry has learnt to vie with the plastic arts in its appeal to the eye and the esthetic sense. That is the reason why Robinson, a master and often a precursor of some of the most significant innovations of poetical technique (short of the eccentric and the risqué), and at the same time a continuator and defender of the tried and approved mental attitude that has always prevailed whenever humanity strove to fulfil its destiny, deserves to be called not merely a classic, but a modern classic—that is one who, while worshipping eternal truths, re-states them in terms of the spirit of the age, in full sympathy with its justifiable and fruitful novelties.

CHAPTER II

POETRY OF EMOTION AND REFLECTION

A CONSIDERABLE part of Robinson's poetry may be termed lyrical—the word being taken in the broad meaning attached to it since modern song has shown that personal effusion is not the only theme that can arouse the emotions.   An ever widening field, including thought as well as passion, has been lately, in America as well as Europe, appropriated by lyrical poetry.   Robinson is one of the modern poets who have extended to far horizons the range of poetical vision and brought into close communion the head and the heart.   I choose, however, to call "poetry of emotion and reflection" those productions of his in which we find intensity of feeling, intellectual enthusiasm, a keen sense of beauty, and a genius for melody, lest the epithet "lyrical," in spite of the extension it has lately received, should seem to imprison him within too narrow boundaries.   For there is novelty, as well as strength of inspiration, in his work. He invested with shapely forms and wrapped in harmony, motives that have been long considered as belonging rather to the sphere of the psychologist than the poet.   But, even when he is most thoughtful, he can be as much of a songster as the lyrists who weave words

34

and metres for the mere delight of the sensibility, the fancy, or the ear.

He does not, it is true, always succeed in keeping his meditative themes within the limits of clear and beautiful expression. He can be so engrossed in his thoughts as to neglect outward form and even fail to take the reader with him through the maze of his subtle notations. This is as much as to say that he does not always reach the perfect balance between matter and manner, or that his inspiration does not always dwell on the summit-line where intellect and art meet in happy accord. But what poet since the day of Homer or Horace, ever showed at his best at all moments and in all moods? We shall not conceal such defects as are to be found in his poems, but they need blind no intelligent reader to the many exquisite beauties.

Robinson's poetical vision strikes us by its concentration. It extends rather in depth than in breadth. His proper domain is the human mind and the human heart; his power of emotion and of reflection applies to life as he knows it from his own experience or from his observation of his fellow-men. His lyrical inspiration (in lyrics proper) does not go back to the historical past; nor is it much attracted by nature, or by any merely exterior or picturesque subject. Nature is present in his work as a background, or a setting, or in the imagery which clothes his thought in concrete vision, or in allegories or symbols. But nature as a motive for descriptions, or for outbursts of esthetic wonder, or as a source of vital energy, hardly retains his attention. Within the realm of human emotion and mental activity, which he makes essentially his own, the scope of his interest is also limited. He seldom indulges in joy, or in playful dallying with pleasant levities, or in gentle musings on the grace of youthful deportment. His view of man's estate is always grave, often melancholy, not unusually sombre. Even his humor is generally sad or grim. It is a one-sided presentation of human nature, but in a line which offers the greatest possibility for earnest thinking and dramatic rendering, which opens itself most favorably to psychological and spiritual insight, and gives the poet the best chance—were it at the risk of a reduced audience—to gain rank among the masters of literature. Robinson has improved the best opportunities tendered him by his temperament, his natural leanings, and his genius for lofty expression, in the rich field of thoughtful experience.

Lyrical poetry, however varied its objects, generally presents itself as dominated by Self. The writer feels intensely, gives free scope to the movements of his sensibility, listens to the gentle murmuring, or the loud appeals, of passion within himself, or reacts to the stimuli of affective life outside, and pours forth his feelings in rhythmical utterance. This is true of most lyrical poets, and it is true in part of Robinson. There must be a personal element in lyrical poetry, or it would remain cold and artificial, possess only the outward shell, not the substance, of inspiration. As Robinson's lyrics, at their best, are glowing with emotion and throbbing with sincerity, there is no doubt that his soul is in them. He certainly belongs to the sacred tribe of the inspired, in whose hearts the wailings and railings of human anguish reverberate with tenfold echo. But it is not frequently the vicissitudes of his own feelings that he voices in his verse. Never was lyrical poet so little of an egotist. He entrusts various characters—some of whom he may have actually known, others who are creations of his fancy—with the expression of a wide range of emotional experience. Even when he speaks in his own name, it is often to relate facts of the soul that came within his observation as he gazed on life's spectacle and contemplated men's illusions and disillusions. His characters are not replicas, under different personalities, of the same type that might be traced up to himself. They have their own idiosyncrasies, imprinted in them by their way of life, their calling, their temper, and their destiny. Robinson possesses to the highest degree the faculty of sympathy, which, together with his psychological acumen, gives him an unwonted insight into the secrets of the human soul. His poetical genius is primarily dramatic, but (in the poems we are considering) associated with a lyrical fervor akin to that which we find in the high-strung passages or the songs of Shakespeare. I make bold to use the epithet "Shakespearian," because in tragic lyric dialogue or soliloquy, impassioned narrative or heart-true confidence, Robinson, when he is truly himself, shows a power of probing the depths of the soul, connecting outward attitude with inner mood, heightening thought by images, creating wonder, evoking mystery, and enhancing the materials

37

of experience and emotion by the magic of words, which bears the unmistakable mark of great poetical creation.

Some American critics attribute Robinson's propensity to dwell on the mournful aspects of life to his puritan ancestry and education. A few, obsessed by their desire to rescue America, as they think, from the blight of puritanism, denounce him as a stickler to the spirit of self-distrust and self-repression which for so many years cramped American literature and art, and their prejudice prevents them from doing justice to his intellectual acuteness and exquisite artistry. Others, blinded by their exclusive loyalty to Walt Whitman and the form of art derived from him, do not admit that great poetry can be produced outside the pale of the new faith. Narrow-mindedness of this kind is responsible for the late anathema that branded Robinson as a "futilitarian"—which might be taken as libellous, if it was not simply meaningless. With due attention to what Whitman has done to renew and enrich American poetry, to his forceful and aggressive personality and to his spirited interpretation of American buoyancy, brawn, and brag; with due recognition of the stimulus he furnished to the New World to articulate its national self-consciousness, and even to the Old World to adopt new points of view and formulas, one must not fall into the exaggeration of identifying Whitman's crude appeal with the whole voice of America. He expressed the muscular and exuberant optimism of American democracy and deserved to be redeemed from the unjustified neglect from which he had long suffered. But the reaction against old injustice must not blind the present generation to other permanent and significant features of the American genius. Robinson is no less distinctly American, from a different point of view, and his Americanism is no less vigorous and genuine than some loud and boisterous varieties embedded in the Whitmanian heritage.

According to the doctrine of the literature of revolt, the quality of "Puritan" is associated with unpleasant notions, which preclude a just acknowledgment of the intellectual complexities that may be comprised under the name. The Puritan of old hardly survives to-day. The narrow, precise, prudish, and captious spirit, connected with theological intolerance, and the blue laws, is only to be found (and with notable attenuations) among remote communities where culture, artistic progress and scientific knowledge have not penetrated. With this antiquated spirit of cant and bigotry, Robinson is as professedly at variance as the free lances of the New York intelligentsia. He expressed his disapproval of it, in his own discreet, detached manner, whose moderation and reserve do not blur the plain intent. He left no doubt as to his convictions and sympathies, when he described Tilbury village and the hypocritical way in which the people, of one accord, tried quietly to suppress poor Captain Craig, son of Bohemia and disciple of Epicurus.

There was just a false note in the Tilbury tune . . .
They might have made him sing by feeding him
Till he should march again, but probably
Such yielding would have jeopardized the rhythm;

39

They found it more melodious to shout
Right on, with unmolested adoration,
To keep the tune as it had always been,
To trust in God, and let the Captain starve.

In the same, or a similar, village, one Flammonde, born and bred abroad, of startling elegance and perfect unconcern for puritan prejudices, creates a sort of scandal, not by any misconduct, but by his very qualities of refined taste, quick intelligence and human sympathy. By such indirect, yet unmistakable means, Robinson intimates where he stands in the conflict between the forces of the past and of the present. He denies nothing of the legacy of tradition which has kept its value, but, at the crossing of the roads, steps firmly into the paths of the modern spirit.

A breath from the open passed over America in the second half of the XIXth century. Under the impulse of liberal-minded thinkers and writers, and in the light of philosophical and literary influences, native or foreign, there has developed a type of *modernized* Puritan, that has preserved the best of the sturdy qualities of the Fathers, while discarding their narrow views and offensive limitations. The modern Puritan no longer despises the world or considers this vale of tears as a mere place of penance where sinful man makes himself fit for the life to come, although he still cherishes longings for a high moral and spiritual ideal. He no longer wastes his mental energy in torturing himself by horrible visions of eternal punishment, although he remains true to the worship of the conscience. He is too alive to the unity of the cosmos and the universality of Nature's laws not to make allowance for the passions, that are part of the Life-Force, although he still makes a difference in degree between the irresponsible rush of the instincts and the conscious activity of the higher will. He retains a grave and reflective attitude towards the doings of man, that leads him to exercise his judgment and believe in the power of volition to guide our behavior and regenerate our moral being enmeshed in the toils of doubt or tossed by blind impulses.

With Robinson, this elevation and liberality of the moral life associates itself with intellectual earnestness, applied to the observation of the ways of the world, the appraisal of the motives of action and the relations of men to their social surroundings. Hence his psychological insight and his ability to weigh moral values. Far from restraining his width of ken, it breaks down the barriers of self and opens to him the vast field of universal contemplation. The passions are not banned from his outlook, but find their appropriate place in a well-balanced life-scheme. If the poet's reading of man's habitual ways is not often cheerful, the reason is not a perverse narrowing of the scope of action, but the constant comparison between the transient and permanent values. This very seriousness, associated as it is with the power of emotion, makes for the pathetic quality of his verse. If he does not complacently deal with the carnal aspects of the sex problems, he gains in intellectuality what he loses in sensuality, and avoids the morbid obsession of sex which mars much of recent American literature, under the questionable influence of Baudelaire and Zola. His reserve does not un-

duly restrict the field of his scrutiny, for he claims all
the rest of the vast domain of human emotions. The
range and intensity of his lyrical inspiration is a decisive
proof that he has chosen the wiser part.

Robinson is true to another precedent of American
literary tradition by his culture and his mastery of the
technique of verse. While rejecting the timidities of
the imitative school, he retains the humanistic allegiance and the finished workmanship of the American
classics. Culture does not imply imitation. With
Robinson, it means the perfect training of the intellect,
the sense of balance and of proportion, the avoidance
of verbosity and redundancy. This terseness of thought
and of phrase appears especially in his admirable handling of the sonnet—the test *par excellence* of the cultivated genius. By the rare union of creative power and
disciplined composition, he achieves the feat of affirm-
ing his originality, while keeping the connection with
the pleiad of American cultured poets in the past.

Robinson's poems of emotion and reflection are mostly
drawn from three great lyrical sources: love, death and
the ideal. We shall deal with each of these main themes,
trying to penetrate, as we analyze them, the nature of
the poet's intellect and sensibility, the range of his
observation and of his sympathy, and his outlook on life,
the world and human destiny.

The first published collection of poems, *The Children
of the Night,* in 1897, when the author was twenty-eight,
already shows him in full possession of his mature

thought and of his means of expression. It contains a slightly greater proportion of smooth verse and polished stanzas than his later volumes. He seems to take pleasure in inditing melodious rhymes in the sweet old-French forms of the *ballade* and *villanelle*. These dainty experiments in song were for him mere exercises in technique, by which he tested his skill in rhyming and difficult stanza-building. He was to retain, on the other hand, two poetical forms, in which he evinced from the first perfect mastery, the sonnet and the (English) ballad, especially the latter as enabling him to mingle in one poem story, dramatic design and thoughtful observation. The traditional ballad, composed of four-line stanzas with alternating rhymes, easily extends into a derivative form, half-way between the ballad and the ode, with stanzas of five, six, or seven lines, and a complex rhyme-scheme. He vies in these verse-forms with the Renaissance poets, as he rivals them in the sonnet,—with this difference that, whereas the XVIth century poets expressed pastoral tenderness and described enchanted bowers, he treats psychological and meditative subjects, without losing the warmth of emotion or the glow of sensuous beauty. In this first publication of a young man, there are no subjective effusions of love, which young poets are so prompt to indulge in. Love occurs as a motive, but treated objectively, as by an observer of life and a student of the passions, bent on seizing on the wing the spirit of man's rapture or anguish.

Disappointed love haunts him with its insistent

43

pathos. But he does not let his characters burst out in distracted ravings or mope in despair. In the drama of passion, he feels attracted by the fortitude of the strong or by the gentle dreaming of the idealists. He does not indulge in mere story-telling: there is hardly ever any story in his poems. Through a dimly delineated narrative, the emotion and its intellectual or ideal reverberation come forth with striking vividness. The characters have often no name: they stand for universal man, strongly individualized by the circumstances of the case.

In *Her Eyes*, a gifted painter, who has reached the summit of fame, feels his life blighted because he could not win the woman he loved. The world rang with his praise,

> But he cloaked his triumph, and searched, instead,
>> Till his cheeks were sere and his hairs were gray.
> "There are women enough, God knows," he said . . .
>> "There are stars enough—when the sun's away."

No arguing with himself could assuage his grief. He painted from memory the face of the cruel one, trying over and over again to render the expression of her eyes.

> But he wrought them at last with a skill so sure
>> That her eyes were the eyes of a deathless woman,—
> With a gleam of heaven to make them pure,
>> And a glimmer of hell to make them human.

His life-thoughts were absorbed in the contemplation of that portrait. The form of the poem is in the early manner, characterized by balanced sentences and regular—rather too regular—metrical beats. But the glow of ideal love and the melancholy of balked devotion have the arresting quality of the poet's thoughtful pathos.

In the sonnet, *The Story of the Ashes and the Flame,* a repeatedly deceived lover opens his arms again, with tireless indulgence, to the fickle woman when she comes back to him

> with penitent scared eyes
> That had in them the laughter of the moon
> For baffled lovers.

The symbol of the "ashes and the flame" is delicately woven in this story of sad experience, with a sure sense of the poetical beauty which a concrete image adds to the delineation of the movements of the soul. We shall see later what powerful use the poet makes of this means of heightening the emotion by the imaginative blending of the material and the immaterial.

Baffled passion, turned to ashes, but out of which the disappointed lover, desperately clinging to elusive hope, endeavors to revive a flickering flame, is a motive that attracts the poet as a pathetic proof of the stubbornness of misplaced idealism. In *Eros Turannos,* the character is a woman. She sees through the miserable lies and deceits of her husband.

> But what she meets and what she fears
> Are less than are the downward years,
> Drawn slowly to the foamless weirs
> Of age, were she to lose him.

45

GOSHEN COLLEGE LIBRARY

Here the later form of the poet prevails, with its subtle interweaving of intellectuality and feeling, in a musical flow of plain words, chosen for their expressive simplicity. The emotion culminates in the last stanza, where the poet voices his keen sympathy for suffering lovers:

> . . . for they
> That with a god have striven,
> Not hearing much of what we say,
> Take what the god has given;
> Though like waves breaking it may be,
> Or like a changed familiar tree,
> Or like a stairway to the sea
> Where down the blind are driven.

The vision has a firm intellectual quality, assuming through the images, in spite of the lack of a story, an inevitable force of emotion.

The lack of a story, here, gives freer range to the thoughtful elements of the poem. Elsewhere, as in *Luke Havergal,* it helps create an impression of mystery. Raising an atmosphere of mystery is one of the great achievements of poetry, effected only when the poet, penetrating through imaginative insight into the region of the subconscious, feels his way to strange experience where the actual and the inactual are merged in the chiaroscuro of extra-sensuous perception. Luke Havergal is made to hear a ghostly voice, while he stands there with us in the world of living beings. The scene is made probable by his soul-distraction, born of heart-

46

rending anguish. He is thrown into a state of hallucination.

The facts that are necessary as a foundation for the unwonted happenings are introduced by a method for which Robinson himself suggests, in the title of one of his poems, the term "inferential." From the nature of the disturbance which agitates Luke Havergal's mind, we infer he is a bereaved lover, so upset by sorrow and despair that he is haunted by the thought of suicide. His morbid yearning to recover his lost beloved gets exteriorized, as happens in such cases of emotional madness, and he hears a voice from beyond the grave calling him to the trysting place. It will be at the hour of sunset, in the fall of the year, near the western gate.

> There where the vines hang crimson on the wall.

The voice comes clearer and clearer to him and, in the last stanza, (where every word is a weird repetition of forms expressed before) the effect of wonder, through the association of melancholy beauty and mournful thoughts, reaches its climax.

> There is the western gate, Luke Havergal,
> There are the crimson leaves upon the wall.
> Go, for the winds are tearing them away,—
> Nor think to riddle the dead words they say,
> Nor any more to feel them as they fall;
> But go, and if you trust her she will call.
> There is the western gate, Luke Havergal,
> Luke Havergal.

47

Melancholy + sadness

There may be here a reminiscence of Edgar Poe, as the repetitions and the burden seem to hint. But the beauty of the piece is of a different quality from that which we find in *The Raven* or in *Ulalume*. The interest rests on the inner pathos, not on an outer machinery of supernatural apparitions. Love and death are the themes, but there is nothing of the ghastly horror which generally surrounds Poe's treatment of the subjects. Death, as one of the motives of Robinson's poetry, never appears accompanied by uncanny paraphernalia, or blood-curdling circumstances. It is not described as the dark threshold to a realm of fearful visions. What interests him is the melancholy which falls on things or the sadness that invades feeling hearts on the occasion of death, or the soul-complexities that accompany its approach, or the passionate tumult that it may bring about. In presence of death, Robinson remains the poet of emotion and reflection; he does not lapse into crude or spectacular description, where the external world shuts out the inner action of the feelings. It is the feelings, not the outward accidents, that count here, as in his general conception of life and poetry.

An old man, living in a solitary farm-house, lost his aged wife and dug for her a grave in the forest: Robinson commemorated in a touching sonnet the pity of this expected, but none the less painful, bereavement. There is a sadness about the end of a human existence whether it is that of a plain farmer's wife, like Amaryllis, or that of an obscure wood-ranger like Stafford, whose cabin, after he had disappeared (probably murdered),

48

stands desolate on the mountain slope, wrapt in mournful mystery.

An apple tree that's yet alive saw something, I suppose,
Of what it was that happened there, and what no mortal
    knows.

The very simplicity with which the poet tells his
sympathy gives it a penetrating force. In the little
poem, *Cortège,* the plain wording takes on a musical
wistfulness by the recurrence of two or three lines of
gentle lamentation, like the leading-bars of a funeral
march. We know nothing of the two characters, except that the man and woman loved each other dearly,
and died together "fifteen hundred miles away," in an
accident, maybe, or of the same contagious illness. No
matter: the mystery of this fateful blow comes as a
strange thrill, superadded to the mystery of death.

The pathos reaches a higher accent when the poet
sets in motion complex feelings and stirs deep thoughts,
in connection with death. Thus in *Partnership.*
As usual, there is no tale, no description of the characters, no *exposé* of the circumstances, except what
gleams from a few words fallen from a dying mouth.
We infer that an artist's wife, on her death-bed, being
shown her husband's masterpiece, lately completed, recognizes his genius which she had doubted:

    Yes, you have it; I can see.
    Beautiful . . .
    Lift it where the beams are bright,
    Hold it where the western light,

Shining in above my bed,
Throws a glory on your head.
Now it is all said.

When the feelings are so tense, the simplest words will
convey the greatest emotion. Robinson does not consider it the poet's part, in his tragi-lyric poetry, to startle
or dazzle by a galaxy of brilliant epithets or a diamond-
net of highly wrought sentences. He places himself
in direct contact with the characters, re-constructs their
state of mind by his power of sympathy, gives to each
feeling and thought their proper expression and emphasis, and lets the plain words, welling up straight
from the heart, do their office without any further in-
tervention.

When he speaks in his own name as in *The Whip,* re-
flecting on the tragedy of violent death caused by excess of sorrow, his verse may run into puzzling intricacies
of meaning, while keeping its interior simplicity of
phrase and its power of pathetic, mysterious emotion.
Each clause, carrying its full load of sense, suggests
a complex aspect of the characters' lives or reveals a
whole train of feelings. We uneasily grope our way
through the first reading: it is only a second attentive
perusal which yields the fullness of the contents. Such
poems are not meant for careless or indolent readers:
but great poetry ought not to be approached with indo-
lence or carelessness. The author wants us to collaborate and play our part of interpretation, without which
we should not be worthy of the trust he places in us.

10039

He disdains to draw in solid relief the frame of facts
that might unduly absorb our attention and plunge us
in the vulgarity of a news-item. In a Rembrandt-like
manner of opposed lights and shadows, he limns the
lineaments of the psychical life and the outstanding
features of the soul-drama. The mental picture arises
from the chequered strokes and over-lapping tints,
until each element announces its full individual and
relative value. The seeming obscurity is but a super-
ficial aspect due to the compactness of the design and
the serried manner of the drawing. The very effort
it requires from the reader adds to the quality of the
enjoyment. It is only when we have conquered the
outward difficulty and possessed ourselves of the inner
meaning, that we may pass the portal and enter the
sanctuary. Robinson addresses a public of initiates. The initiation is in itself a culture. The keen intellectual and emotional pleasure is the reward.

In *The Whip*, the stifling gloom of death gives the
psychological drama, compressed in a few short stanzas,
a breathless poignancy. The poet stands by the bier
of a man, who, as we learn from gradual disclosures,
drowned himself after having sounded the depths of
despair. He was a jilted husband, racked by his jealous
suspicions of his wife, making himself miserable by the
pains he took to secure the certainty of his misfortune.
Yet he could not wrench himself from the grip of his
unhappy love:

> The doubt you fought so long,
> The cynic net you cast,

> The tyranny, the wrong,
> The ruin, they are past;
> And here you are at last,
> Your blood no longer vexed.
> The coffin has you fast,
> The clod will have you next.

His wife and her paramour, either harrowed by the fear of scandal, or under the husband's threat of some terrible punishment, or urged by the ghastly desire of death that haunts guilty lovers, rushed to the river one day, bent on putting an end to their lives, or driven to it by the husband's mad pursuit. He followed or chased them to the brink, and, after seeing them hurl themselves headlong to death, plunged after them. Drawn by some ghoulish lure? Spurred by grief? Maddened by remorse? The mystery of the case assumes weird concreteness in the poet's mind, and he seems to see it materialize in a strange sign, a bruise that was discovered on the dead man's face. Is not this mysterious mark like a whip-stroke dealt by some unknown agency?

> There were some ropes of sand
> Recorded long ago,
> But none, I understand,
> Of water. Is it so?
> And she—she struck the blow, . . .
> You saw the river flow —
> Still, shall I call you blind?

It was not the welt of a physical blow. Was it a wound inflicted by spirit on spirit? Pathos and mystery meet in this symbol.

52

The poet's versatility and wide range of inspiration
appear in the fact that he can return from such a poignant drama of grief and death to the gentle melancholy
that hovers, like the tang of fallen leaves, about the
quiet passing away of a guileless soul. The subdued
emotion called up by peaceful death, in a setting of
beauty, imparts to a sonnet, entitled *Souvenir,* so much
pervading grace and wistfulness, that it remains forever imprinted on our memory. It shows the poet's
power to create a living vision out of the simplest materials. The remembrance of a country house, in the
middle of a garden, seen once by the poet when a child,
hushed in the silence that surrounds a death-bed—it
is all, and these simple data inspire him with one of
his most beautiful, touching, and melodious short
lyrics.

A vanished house that for an hour I knew
By some forgotten chance when I was young
Had once a glimmering window overhung
With honeysuckle wet with evening dew.
Along the path tall dusky dahlias grew,
And shadowy hydrangeas reached and swung
Ferociously; and over me, among
The moths and mysteries, a blurred bat flew.

Somewhere within there were dim presences
Of days that hovered and of years gone by.
I waited, and between their silences
There was an evanescent faded noise;
And though a child, I knew it was the voice
Of one whose occupation was to die.

Beauteous things here are touched to sacred splendor
by the mysterious presence of Eternity. Eternity opens
to love and death the gates of the infinite, or closes the
avenues of life and thumps the heavy lid of the tomb
over nothingness. Does death achieve the liberation of
the spirit? Or is life, with its grievous burden of disappointments and its fleeting gleams of hope, the brief
flickering of an unsteady flame? Such problems are
proper objects of meditation for a thoughtful poet, born
of a religious ancestry, brought up in the cultured atmosphere of New England and inclined by his own
temperament to dwell on the weightiest questions that
thrust themselves on man's cogitation. A large part
of Robinson's poetry is philosophical. The thinker and
the poet coöperate to produce works that are profound
without losing their beauty or their pathetic quality.
Indeed, it is in some of his meditative poems that Robinson's genius yields its fairest fruitage.

In the hands of this perfect artist, who puts in the
treatment of the great lyric themes—love and death,
passion and grief, yearning or regret—so much tenderness, depth of feeling, dramatic force, richness of coloring and sweetness of melody, philosophical poetry is in
no danger of falling into didactic dryness or cold liter-
ality. In his meditative mood, he approaches the subjects that retrace the life of the spirit and man's highest
aspirations with his full emotivity, visionariness and
magic of phrase. Let us not do him the ill service to
insist on his doctrine. It is not his theoretical tenets

(if he has any) that make themselves vocal in his work, but his humanity. As a cultured man and a well-balanced thinker, he is neither a mystic nor a sceptic, neither a romantic dreamer nor a morose pessimist, but an observer of the facts of the spirit as well as of physical realities, who knows man's limitations and weaknesses and yet believes in man's destiny and in life's ideal completion. He is an idealist, who remains attached to Christian feelings, without being hampered by Christian dogma. Emerson must have had an influence over him, rather by his spiritual fervor than by his actual teaching. After all, Robinson harks back to Shakespeare, being keenly alive, like the poet of *The Tempest,* to the splendor of our higher nature, and sadly sensitive, like Prospero, to our inability to rise to the height of our aspirations. For a man of delicate fibre, the tragic disproportion between our longings and our achievements is the source of exquisite pain. This explains that Robinson rather dwells on the tragedy of defeat than on the complacent illusions of proclaimed victory. His artistic purpose is in accord with his philosophical outlook: for it is in the sincere and obstinate, but often frustrated, efforts of man to realize his better self, that dramatic emotion lies. His greatness resides in having brought into vivid light the nobleness of man's endeavor, even when the results stop short of the intentions. In fact, his best philosophical lyrics bear on what has been called "the success of failure." Thereby he shows himself a perfect dramatic poet, as well as a penetrating interpreter of the deeper significance of man's destiny.

He does not belong to any definite philosophical school, in his poems of reflection, any more than he expresses limited individual feelings, in his poems of emotion. He is interested in the vast drama of spiritual life, excluding only from the range of his sympathy the indifference, callousness or gross materialism of the sensual or the unthinking. His poetry is classic—that is universally human—in its essence, while vibrating with the pulse of modern emotivity and resplendent with the glow of modern coloring. He accomplishes the feat of uniting the gorgeousness of vivid tints and the sober purity of sculptural outlines. His imagery flames with the splendors of a rich palette and his style bears the mark of attic preciseness, poise and reserve.

In his first collection of verse, non-content to give perfect specimens of that difficult verse-form, the sonnet, he seems to have exercised himself in the arduous practice of high-pitched expression by composing octaves on philosophical themes. They are unrhymed, most sparing of the graces that reside in simile or metaphor, and yet the exact choice of words, the freshness arising from the novel association of terms, the vigorous concentration of thought associated with the compactness of phrase—besides the elasticity and forcible beat of the rhythm—give these philosophical epigrams an irresistible strength and charm. A few lines borrowed from some of the octaves will, we think, justify our statement.

I.   We thrill too strangely at the master's touch;
     We shrink too sadly from the larger self; . . .
                 . . . we do not feel—
     We dare not feel it yet—the splendid shame
     Of uncreated failure . . .

IV.   We think
     We are great warriors now, and we can brag
     Like Titans; but the world is growing young,
     And we, the fools of time, are growing with it:—
     We do not fight to-day, we only die;
     We are too proud of death, and too ashamed
     Of God, to know enough to be alive.

In the same volume, the last sonnet, *L'Envoi,* offers the same terseness with more melody in the arrangement of sounds:

     Now in a thought, now in a shadowed word,
     Now in a voice that thrills eternity,
     Ever there comes an onward phrase to me
     Of some transcendent music I have heard.

Such thoughtful rhythmical utterance carries a full share of delight and of deep meaning; yet it is only an attempt by which the poet makes sure of his power of expression. His later productions contain the same condensed exactness and musical quality, with a richer vision. In *The Pilot,* for instance, the poet describes the mystic voyage of fervent souls in search of the light. They have lost their pilot—who died perhaps of too intent thinking—but they are still inspired by his invisible presence. Abstract thought and imagery combine in pathetic emotion.

> From the Past and Unavailing
> Out of cloudland we are steering:
> After groping, after fearing,
> Into starlight we come trailing,
> And we find the stars are true.
> Still, O comrade, what of you?
> You are gone, but we are sailing,
> And the old ways are all new.

The Garden sets forth in a startling allegory the dependence of man on God's guidance. God, the gardener, leads man to a plot of wasted ground where his fruitless acts are piled up in a heap of weeds:

> And they were like a book that I could read,
> Whose every leaf, miraculously signed,
> Outrolled itself from Thought's eternal seed,
> Love-rooted in God's garden of the mind.

Allegory takes a fuller form in *The Town Down the River*. The four parts of the poem present, through the phantasmagoria of a vision, as many phases of the pageant of life. Separate groups of people, one after the other, pass along a road skirting the river which leads to the Town, further below, whose lure exerts on them an irresistible attraction. They are stopped, one after the other, by the Watcher by the Way, who tries to keep them away from the false lights and spurious disportments of the Town—but in vain. The boy and the

maiden, who trip along in love ecstasy, rebuff the withered sage disdainfully. The strong men, in the full
bloom of ripe manhood, gently ward him off. "To the
slower folk who stumbled, To the weak and world-
humbled," the Watcher addresses an urgent appeal—as
useless as before. Lastly come the aged and decrepit,
"shrunken and claw-fingered," who can no longer hear
the call of the bewitching Town down the River; they
have been too severely scalded by experience to wish to
meet there new disappointments. This time, it is the
wise Watcher, as old as they, but less disillusioned who
goads them on and takes them along with him down the
way the others are treading. For the aged sage himself has felt the urge of Life and follows in the footsteps
of the enamored, the strong and the stubborn, where a
resistless force drags men to their fate. The short lines
and the brief stanzas carry with them a lightness and
speed which suggests the coursing of the blood and the
beating of the heart, as men hustle on the race to happiness or to destruction. The allegory develops along
the lines of its inner logic, like a vision that unrolls
before the mind's eye, without any interpretative aside,
yet with a clearness and force which vividly brings out
the hidden meaning. There dwells in the poem a pathos
that equals at times that of Shelley's *Triumph of Life,*
but retrieved by a bracing faith in action, which removes
all taint of romantic despair and sounds with a true
American ring. The melancholy of the Watcher's
warning is baffled by the tripping rhythm and the chim-
ing rhymes. The pathos of the feelings, the grave

59

M. A. Sky

humor of the tone, the power of dramatic visionary construction, the sure sense of the deep meaning of Life, make up an arresting whole, to which few intelligent readers can remain indifferent. Even if the general public were loath to make the intellectual effort that gives the key to the translucent allegory, the poet could not but be satisfied that he has attained, through subtle magic of thought and expression the noble goal of high imaginative creation.

There remained for him to transcend the plane of allegorical vision and rise to the supreme excellence of the symbol. In the symbol, there is no mere juxtaposition of a concrete image and an abstract idea, but an actual blending of the material and the immaterial in a momentary triumph of the spirit. Robinson achieved this conquest in *The Man Against the Sky*. His aim, here, was to compress in four hundred lines, the theme that Dante treated in the third part of his sacred epic. Without instituting a comparison, which the author in his modesty would not admit, we do not hesitate to affirm that there is Dantesque majesty and grandeur in the poem, with an originality of vision and a modernity of thought that remove any suspicion of unconscious imitation. Averse as the poet is to egotism and romantic subjectivity, he takes for his hero, not himself or a duplicate of himself, but a human being without a name, age or distinctive features, that stands for universal man, facing the mystery of the beyond, in a glowing radiation of unearthly splendor.

The coloring has the bold and rich imaginative quality

how symbol from different is allegory?

of the prophetic books, and it assumes rare solemnity from the sense of awe which permeates its texture. Although there is little trace of orthodox belief, religious fervor forms the leading inspiration, with all the force of self-reliance and strenuous individualism that marks the puritan temper:

> Even he who climbed and vanished may have taken
> Down to the perils of a depth not known,
> From death defended though by men forsaken,
> The bread that every man must eat alone.

What are the thoughts that agitate this man, thus "moving along the molten west," onward to a goal of glory or an abyss of self-annihilation? The poet passes in review the moods that may take hold of his mind and is thus led to express the purport of the philosophical solutions concerning life and death which divide the modern world. Does the man approach the great riddle with self-complacency or cynical scepticism? Too proud to keep the old faith, does he fall into the grip of fear or armor himself in grim stubbornness? Does he form the ambitious design to build a new certainty on reason and science, or does he blind himself by the illusion that earthly greatness is the proper goal of man's endeavor? Such are the musings through which the poet allows his mind to wander as he beholds the wayfarer, "black-drawn against wild red."

What matters here is less what point of doctrine may lie at the base of one or the other attitude, than the feelings which are involved in it. It is the soul-drama that the poet grasps, as it arises from the conflict between cowardly abandon and earnest striving, reason and faith, self-seeking and self-sacrifice, humility and pride. He scrutinizes the human heart in its secret nooks and corners, exposes its weaknesses, delusions, or idle boasts with relentless severity, tears the veil of unconfessed lies, pricks swollen pride, bends haughty brows—not indifferent or unmoved, but letting out his pity or indignation in accents of throbbing or scathing irony. The acuteness of the remarks, the novelty of the illustrations, the sharp contrasts, the aptness and richness of phrase, the atmosphere of symbolical remoteness that wraps the whole, raise the poem to an unwonted quality of philosophical and lyrical beauty. The expression of ideas may now and then be too abstract and a few periods too intricate for perfect clearness, but generally the thought flows in smooth musical lines, suffused with the glow of bright imagery.

The egoist treads the soil of the sacred hill, haloed in self-satisfaction. He has done well in life, secured possession of the good things of the earth and spreads his proprietorship over the world, regardless of others, unmindful of the generations which have opened the way:

> Why question of his ease of who before him,
> In one place or another where they left
> Their names as far behind them as their bones,
> And yet by dint of slaughter, toil and theft,
> And shrewdly sharpened stones,

Carved hard the way for his ascendency
Through deserts of lost years?

The cynic grins his contemptuous smile at man's
achievements, religious creeds and even the splendors
of the universe, in his blind fury of negation:

He may have been a player without a part,
Annoyed that even the sun should have the skies
For such a flaming way to advertise;
He may have been a painter sick at heart
With Nature's toiling for a new surprise; . . .
He may have proved a world a sorry thing
In his imagining,
And life a lighted highway to the tomb.

The ruined magnate, bending under the weight of
disappointed ambition, looks upon the glory of the incandescent heavens as "the abysmal conflagration of his
dreams." As for those who have no hope in the progress
of our race, no faith in the spirit toiling upward through
the efforts of generations, what need have they, the poet
asks himself,

For launching other lives to voyage again
A little farther into time and pain, . . .
Why . . . hunger through another season
To find out why 'twere better late than soon
To go away and let the sun and moon
And all the silly stars illuminate
A place for creeping things,
And those that root and trumpet and have wings,
And herd and ruminate,

> Or dive and flash and poise in rivers and seas,
> Or by their loyal tails in lofty trees
> Hang screeching lewd victorious derision
> Of man's immortal vision?

Through this bitter irony, the poet imparts his faith and his hope by indirection. But he is not satisfied with meeting the scoffers on their own ground. He affirms his trust in the ideal, which upholds man through the struggle of life and keeps him afloat in the midst of storms above the welter of dire conflicts, away from the pangs of despondency. To those who seek truth and keep their courage, Time brings a spiritual reward worth more than power or gold:

> There's more to be known of his harvesting
> When Time the thresher unbinds the sheaves.

In spite of all the turmoil and din of this noisy world, too apt to lose itself in idle agitation and waste its energy in fruitless wranglings, there still rings a note on high which the trained ear can perceive and which, although not of this world, can tame the wild onrush of lust and greed and bathe the spirit in pure harmony:

Nor jewelled phrase nor mere mellifluous rhyme
Reverberates aright, or ever shall,
One cadence of that infinite plain-song
Which is itself all music. Stronger notes
Than any that have ever touched the world
Must ring to tell it—ring like hammer-blows,
Right-echoed of a chime primordial,
On anvils, in the gleaming of God's forge. (XIXth Octave)

Such a glowing and ringing expression of the passion for higher truth cannot recur many times in one poet's verse. After having sung his hymn to the glory that dwells in spiritual aspiration and in the feeling nearest to supernal ecstasy—poetical enthusiasm—Robinson does his work of an interpreter of man's life, yet without diverting his eyes from the light that dawns beyond the darkness of this world. It is the implied idealism, present in many of his poems on love or death or the soul-drama, that gives them their elevation and their strength of appeal. Even when he seems absorbed for the nonce in the maze of psychological complexities or in the *détours* of human sorrow, his gravity, his gentle confidence, his wistful thoughtfulness—wherein lies the noble quality of his verse—arise from his habitual intercourse with lofty visions. From the same source derive, for the greatest part, the simple dignity of his diction, the winsomeness of his phrase, the splendor of his imagery, the suggestiveness of his symbolism, the sweetness of his rhythmical or rhymed utterance. His defects are occasional over-refinement, intellectual elusiveness and indulgence in cryptography. But much of his so-called obscurity can be seen through by those who take pains to enter into his inner meaning and make themselves familiar with his ways of expression. What remains is negligible when one considers the bulk, greatness, and beauty of his production. As a lyric poet, he has the richness and sincerity of emotion, the dramatic force, the depth of penetration and of sympathy, the power of vision and of transcendency, the musical mellowness and charm, that are the privilege of the masters of song, and to those gifts of the sensibility, of the intellect, and of artistic perception, he adds the classic touch of universality. I feel confident that the best of his lyrics will be recorded in later times in the Golden Treasury of modern classics in the English language.

CHAPTER III

Treatment of the Arthurian Legend

DID Robinson, we may ask ourselves, when he felt attracted by the legend of Arthur as a source of rich human material and of noble poetry, think of the interdict pronounced by Walt Whitman?   Did he pause to consider the emphatic dismissal signified by the bard of Camden to the King of Camelot and his court?

Vanished the turrets that Usk from its waters reflected,
Arthur vanished with all his knights—Merlin, Lancelot,
    Galahad, all gone, dissolved utterly like an exhalation!
Pass'd! pass'd! for us forever pass'd, that once so mighty
    world, now void, inanimate, phantom world!

If Robinson thought of this passage, he did not take its naïve and sonorous rhetoric as the final pronouncement on the heroes who loom through the haze of the old legend.   He certainly, on the other hand, did realize the difficulty of treading on ground that had been explored by Spenser and appropriated by the great Victorians.   But he was not the man to shrink from a task surrounded with peril.   Conscious of having discovered new virtualities of beauty, truth and human pathos in the old tale, he would abstract himself from what had been done before, and set to giving expression to his own sense of the grandeur of the theme, its emotional appeal and symbolic value.

Robinson's strength lies in the psychological insight with which he analyses the characters, and the dramatic force with which he presents the conflict of feelings. These qualities of his—to be found in all his poems dealing with the fluctuations and vicissitudes of the human soul—introduce a valuable addition to the constituents of the story as traditionally treated. The gain is the more to be prized, as it does not preclude other singular beauties—lyrical intensity, sensuous opulence and bold flights of idealistic aspiration. If those merits are not unmixed with shortcomings, let us not forget that unevenness is a fatal contingency to which poets, including those of rarest excellence, are commonly exposed. The *Tristram* and the *Merlin* are, of all his productions, the least tainted by defects; and such blemishes as exist in them are compensated by constant felicity of phrase and imaginative creations of supreme splendor. When matter and manner thus meet in exquisite artistry, criticism is disarmed.

Before approaching Robinson's individual treatment of the Arthurian legend, let us cast a glance at the way in which it was handled by some of his great predecessors. Two English poets of exceptional fame, Tennyson and Swinburne, treated the subject in the latter part of the XIXth century, each with consummate talent, but neither with the vigor or depth of thought which proclaim undisputed mastery.

Tennyson, a true poet by the decorative grace of the

plastic details, the daintiness of the imagery, and the quaint intricacy of the phrasing, yet falls short of greatness by a certain lack of human quality. Making himself the self-ordained herald of Victorian virtue, he belittled a noble matter by a weak allegorical treatment of the episodes and characters. His "pure maidens" and "virgin Knights" will do well as models for pious painters of chapel windows, but they cannot stand the test of criticism probing human truth. All the deeds and thoughts that meet approval at the court of his King Arthur wear the varnish of glazed respectability. Had Tennyson been gifted with true dramatic power and insight, he would have been debarred from using them by the very postulate which conditions the poems—the warriors' and ladies' impenetrability to any touch of passionate ardor. When temptation grazes them, they turn aside with a shudder. And even this shudder discountenances the admirable Arthur, who blushes at it as at a dangerous sign of the presence of sin.

> O my liege and King! (exclaims Merlin)
> O selfless man and stainless gentleman,
> Who wouldst, against thine own eye-witness, fain
> Have all men true and leal, all women pure,
> How, in the mouths of false interpreters,
> Is thy white blamelessness accounted blame!

Lancelot and Guinevere burn for each other with an all but immaterial flame, that would sublimate them into astral bodies, were it not for a pinch of remorse, which ruffles their conscience in spite of their spotless purity. If they happen to ride out alone in the forest, under the leafy cover of the trees, Lancelot's hand is kept from erring to Guinevere's by the falcon perched on it, and, as the poet says,

> Their talk was all of training, terms of art,
> Diet and seeling, jesses, leash and lure.

The "white blamelessness" of such a "supersensual sensual bond," however pleasing to Queen Victoria's modest ears, as a meet homage from her appointed Poet Laureate, did not substantiate the poems with the flesh and blood of human passion.

Tennyson styled his poems "Idylls," whose faint colors and mild tremors dimly gleam against a background of "white samite, mystic, wonderful." He did not intend—shall I say, he was not fitted by the nature of his genius—to search the human soul and rend the veil from the living facts of tragic reality. He told stories, often with delicate ingenuity and rare charm; he wove a glossy fabric of mysterious births and supernatural deaths, chivalrous deeds and innocent loves, prophetic forebodings and magic spells. But he delighted too much in the wonder of heroic adventures and the weirdness of mediaeval lore to dwell on the deep significance of the legend and the blood-red passion which the Celtic bards had poured—maybe unconsciously and not seldom awkwardly—in the veins and arteries of the old narrative. We cannot discover any human truth for the elaborate tracery.

The Idyll entitled *Merlin and Vivien*—which calls for

direct comparison with Robinson's *Merlin*—is not one of the best of the Tennysonian sequence.   The poet may have thought he had achieved success, because he made the piece a sort of abstract of the whole cycle: but this very fact makes the defects more apparent.   Besides, the poem is marred by flaws of its own.   There was an obvious occasion to treat a love episode unhampered by the timid restraints which prevailed in the other Idylls.   We might have had a picture of triumphant passion, with perhaps an ebb and flow of cunning wiles and impetuous assaults on the part of the woman, and with alternate rebuffs and surrenders, tentative resistance and unwilling pliancy on the part of the man, showing a gradual lapse from his eminence as a champion of moral fortitude and intellectual sternness.   But the character of Vivien is endowed with no dignity, not even with the minimum of shrewdness that would have made a low woman (which she was not, considering her rank at court) assume some pretended reserve, to win the good graces of the prophet and sage.   Tennyson is so absorbed in his conventional scheme of opposing Vice and Virtue—Merlin representing full-blown Victorian innocence, and Vivien hateful sin—that he makes the fay a moral monster under her lissome, petulant attractiveness, a mere incarnation of the lure of the flesh.

As soon as she and Merlin landed on the shore of Broceliande and settled to rest, she crept up to him,

> holding by his heel,
> Writhed toward him, glided up his knee and sat;
> Behind his ankle twined her hollow feet

Together, curved an arm about his neck,
Clung like a snake; and letting her left hand
Droop from his mighty shoulder, as a leaf,
Made with her right a comb of pearl to part
The lists of such a beard as youth gone out
Had left in ashes—

It is prettily said, but the quaint dexterity of the expression hardly hides the vulgarity of the situation. Of course, we are made to understand that Vivien is no other than a female fiend, and Merlin, admonishing himself, whispers the word "harlot." But it is Tennyson's weakness not to have set the tone in a higher key, and to have given us (but for the beauty of the verse) a scene as devoid of human complexity as a moralizing fable.

There is no more psychological truth in the rest of the poem. In lieu of an analysis of the feelings, we hear from Merlin's lips marvelous stories: the chase of the hart with the golden horns, the riding by the well that "laughs at iron," the sea-fight of a King with a tawny pirate, the seeking of the wizard with the hairless glassy head, the tale of the Knight with the painted shield (Azure, an Eagle rising or, the Sun/ In dexter chief). Thus heraldry, witchery, chivalry, venery are called in to multiply the incidents and vary the picturesqueness of the piece: but the more skill in the dainty borrowings from outlandish lore, the less human truth in the development of the episode. Vivien sings a song in pretty ternary stanzas, whose intricate conceits and burdens rival Donne's ingenuity. Then she passes in review the scandal of the court, which Merlin indignantly refutes, vindicating the sinlessness of every Knight. When we have wandered through all those digressions, in which we well-nigh lose the thread of the love-contest, a storm suddenly breaks out, a flash of lightning blazes past the couple, and, without any preparation or indeed any reason, Merlin's attitude undergoes an unexpected change. He yields, not his love, but the charm that Vivien had been asking as a boon, and with which she will entomb him in the trunk of an oak.

The poem may be meant as an allegory (and rather awkward at that) of the blackness of evil love. But the desultory conduct of the narrative, the lack of psychological substance and of dramatic interest prevent us from being moved. Under a rich display of verbal effects, the action lags, the feelings are inadequate or vulgar, and the conclusion falls flat.

Swinburne draped in the gorgeous vestment of his golden verse one of the episodes of the Arthurian legend that are the most beautiful and the most replete with human tenderness and pathos, the love of Tristram and Isolt. He cannot be said to have made it a supreme work of art, for his facile genius was too apt to wander when about to reach the high mark of shapely design. Yet as far as his erratic fancy permitted, he did justice to the subject. The poem as a whole does not quite satisfy a fastidious taste, but it contains masterly parts. Tennyson conceived his Idylls in the epic style, with a lack of firmness and virility in the expression of human truth, that detracts from the charm of the smooth flowing narrative. Swinburne's tone is lyric, with occasional passages of dramatic stress rather too much interspersed with sonorous, windy organ-music and an excess of wild imagery.

There is a rich human element in the poem provided by the original data of the old Celtic fable. What new motives he introduced out of his own fund of sensitive or creative imagination often enhance the value of the whole. For instance, he was not content to appropriate the traditional device of the love-potion in its primitive bareness. He gave it its full symbolical strength by causing love to awake in Isolt's and Tristram's hearts before they drank of the fateful cup. This is a felicitous addition to the mediaeval epic, one which is both moving and beautiful, admirably in keeping with the truth of human feelings.

The best parts of the poem are hymns of passionate love. They take on additional beauty from the setting of dawn-hues or sunset-flames, or from the intimate correspondence of the emotions with the varying aspects of the sea. Often too they are diluted in such a flood of diamond beams, silvery clouds, shining grass and star-lit waves, that we faint under this deluge of sweetness and wish some sober Genie might have been present at the poet's birth, and thrown in, among so many bewitching gifts, the sense of measure or indeed mere common sense.

In spite of a decided enrichment of the original story by many a felicitous stroke, Swinburne on the whole remained too much the slave of the old tale. The characters are acted upon from outside, and we do not feel that Fate, which overpowers them, is made to represent the inner forces of the soul or the inevitable logic of the passion. The love of Tristram and of Isolt is static, always the same through the numerous adventures that thwart their eventful lives. Hence, endless and wearisome repetitions of the same lyric themes or elegiac plaints. Conceived as it is, the poem ought to have been written in one thousand, instead of six thousand, lines. The structure of the old tale, it is true, seemed to impose to the modern poet its stiff outlines and rigid bearings; but Swinburne might have repeated the happy changes he introduced in the first Canto. He ought not to have submitted the characters to the impact of external events, without trying to describe their possible inner reactions. Static passion may provide light themes for a short sketch; but it is only dynamic passion, the tragic instability of man's feelings, that can provide material for a noble epic or dramatic work. It is only the union of strong and varied emotion with deep thought that gives rise to masterly art.

Robinson, in his poems borrowed from the Arthurian stock, chose the episodes that might open opportunities for his thoughtful and meditative genius, give full scope to his intellectual insight into character and to his imaginative grasp of symbols, and guide his treatment of the plot and his description of the passions to the vital point of juncture where truth meets beauty. His poems, often as gracefully gentle and softly musical as Tennyson's, and often as fraught with sensuous richness and lyrical splendor as Swinburne's, derive their essential quality from robust thinking, psychological penetration, and pathetic force. He does not need to resort to spells of witches or fairies. His sole supernatural agencies are Time and Fate, that is, awful impersonations of the iron laws of change and of moral retribution. Under the sway of Time and Fate, his characters act according to the inner logic of men's moods, which change as men pass from youth to age, or as they shift from self-seeking to self-sacrifice, from weak indulgence to ideal aspiration, or the reverse. Ever, in Robinson's epics, the reading of life runs on parallel lines with the poetic rendering of the story and the picture of the emotions. He is the first poet, in the history of literature in the English language, who has fully expressed the virtualities of the Arthurian legend in terms of symbolic beauty and human truth.

Robinson presents to us beings who belong to our mortal race, transfigured by legendary remoteness. Their superhuman stature and unwonted gifts simply give them greater capacity to think our thoughts, experience our passions, or suffer our sorrows. Allusions are made to Merlin's wonderful youthfulness, at an age when other men are old, mostly to introduce the symbolical episode of his sudden falling into age, when he awakes from love infatuation. He and Arthur and Tristram and the others rise above the level of trite achievement by an heroic use of the ordinary faculties of the intellect and the sensibility. Their striking appearance or behavior is part of the poetical atmosphere, which

throws a radiance about their persons and the vicissitudes of their destinies, with the effect of both enhancing
the action and magnifying the human emotion. The
Merlin, the *Lancelot* and the *Tristram* are conceived as
human stories, that appeal directly to our sympathy and
move us as representations of life, with a majesty of
attitude and an intensity of feeling, which create an impression of grandeur. This is not ornamental, but deep,
thoughtful, pathetic poetry, with interludes of gentler
inspiration and more restful beauty. The poems are
dramatic narratives, where the externals, however exquisitely drawn, are kept subordinate, while the human
values are thrust to the fore. The essential constituents are the variations and conflicts of feelings that sway
man's nature, now in joy, more often in grief. To search
the conscience, to show the strange working of personal
weakness in noble souls, to trace the interference of fate
(that is, the unforeseen results of unheeded misdoings),
to depict the way of anger and love, loyalty and treason,
hope and despair, constancy or cowardly self-abandon-
ment, with the consequent exultation, dejection, melancholy resignation or radiant resiliency—such are the
leading lines of the development. Robinson, sometimes
with over-nimble minuteness, generally with a penetrating, deep insight into man's inner nature, reveals himself a master of psychological analysis, endowed with
rare power of translating his observations into terms
of symbolical beauty and dramatic emotion.

He is not primarily concerned in the clash of ambitions that cause men to thwart each other's path or to

rush into secret or open wrangles. There are indeed
to be found, in his poems, encounters of desires and oppositions of aims, that raise furious enmities or draw
blood. But they are secondary. The poet takes them
as the traditional elements of the plot and the necessary
ingredients with which to build a background of physical
facts and moral entanglements. He gives to those struc-
tural elements much vividness or charm; but it is not
there that we must look for the original expression of
his main purpose. The core of his work is the inner
drama, the tragedy that takes place in the hearts of
the chief characters. King Arthur racked by spite and
regret, anger and pity, fear and desperation, when he
discovers that his beautiful and beloved queen has
thrown herself in the arms of Lancelot and that his
kingdom, undermined by treason and the maturing consequences of his own faults, is crumbling to naught;
Lancelot fired by love, urged by devotion to his queenly
mistress, or gripped by implacable Fate and called to his
inevitable destiny by the aspirations of his Grail-smit-
ten better self; Guinevere, queen of beauty and seduction, triumphant in the gratification of her wild desire,
suddenly confronted with her lover's sense of the passing of a world and his resolution to seek away from her
the lonely path to the Light; Merlin despairing of the
future of the kingdom he had built by the might of his
wisdom, flying to sensual indulgence, then drawn back
to Camelot by the indestructible ties of his whole life-
work; Tristram and Isolt involved in a terrible conflict
between irresistible passion and reason which foresees a

dire issue—such are the central dramatic themes of the epics. They are noble, inspiring themes. Balked endeavor, thwarted passion, pathetic efforts of self-redressment, pitiful relapses, inward struggle between the conscious and the subconscious, blind groping after truth, defeated aspirations to happiness—of such life-threads is woven the tragedy of hope and disappointment, with such art-materials is built the epic, that Robinson deliberately removes from the smooth field of esthetic prettiness or bland moralizing to the awful realm of human truth and dramatic intensity.

This explains the composition of the poems. They are built like dramas, with an exposition, a knot and a dénouement, each part made up of carefully elaborated dialogues, interspersed with narrative, where noble thought emerges from brilliant coloring and precise characterization. They are epics too, with glowing descriptions, rich imagery, life-like rendering of attitudes and face-expressions, and deep insight into the working of the mind. They are lyrical poems also, hymning soul-ecstasy in rhythmical harmonious lines, or expressing passion in heaving, vigorous accents. And they are philosophical poems, holding aloft, above the welter of earthly struggles, the noble beacon of spiritual idealism.

The plot of the *Merlin* would be a perfect scenario for a play, but for the retrospective IVth and Vth parts, that take us away from Arthur's court, back to the bower of bliss where ten years before Vivian had drawn the seer by the magic of her siren-song. But this departure from the chronological order is so skilfully handled that it makes for dramatic unity. In the Ist part, we hear of the return of Merlin from Brittany in circumstances that excite both wonder and alarm. Is it the living seer that has come back from his self-burial at Broceliande, or his ghost—so changed is his expression and so secret his presence? When his "rumor-laden resurrection" has been accepted as a fact, there hovers still a doubt as to the survival of his moral self. What has become of his far-seeing vision, since he has made himself "a man of dalliance and a sybarite"? It slowly trickles out that Merlin was summoned by the King, as the only person who could give him advice in his pressing need; and all tremble at the recall of the lost councillor, which they interpret as all but an act of despair. They are haunted by dismal fears.

Thus prepared for gloomy happenings, we are the more moved by the interview that takes place between King Arthur and Merlin. Reproaches, regrets, rehearsal of past wrongs and irreparable misdoings are not apt to mend matters. Merlin can only brace the King to face with courage the last battles that are in store for him, and leaves him darkly brooding over the impending downfall:

> No spoken doom
> That ever chilled the last night of a felon
> Prepared a dragging anguish more profound
> And absolute than Arthur, in these hours,
> Made out of darkness and of Merlin's words;
> No tide that ever crashed on Lyonesse

> Drove echoes inland that were lonelier
> For widowed ears among the fisher-folk,
> Than for the King were memories to-night
> Of old illusions that were dead for ever.

In striking contrast to the sombre picture of a court in the decline and a King on the downward slope to destruction, stands the delicately limned crayon of the love-idyll in Broceliande. The setting, the coloring and the texture of passionate feelings are no tame repetition of what great lyrists of love have indited. Robinson's power of creation recalls now Spenser's sense of natural beauties, now Keats' splendor of glowing tints. But he sets the mark of unmistakable originality on the scene by the delicacy, reserve, gentle winsomeness and harmonious plasticity, with which he invests the amorous dialogue. It is less a love duet than a bandying of syllabled sweetnesses, where the intellect is warmed by the heart and the heart enlivened by the intellect. Merlin is no infatuated gray-beard befooled by a pretty hussy; Vivian no giddy damsel in a wanton mood, lavishing cheap caresses. Both keep the decorous behavior that befits the seer's ripe wisdom and the fay's genteel womanhood, without any loss of sprightliness or spontaneity.

Merlin. If I were young, God knows if I were safe,
   Concerning you in green, like a slim cedar,
   As you are now, to say my life was mine—

Vivian. . . . I have eaten to an empty shell,
   After a weary feast of observation

> Among the glories of a tinsel world
> That had for me no glory till you came,
> A life that is no life.

Pertinent characterisation, playful tenderness, a dotting of subdued hues, make of this prelude a dainty miniature, attracting no less by the graceful delineation of costume, complexion and attitude, than by the subtle depicting of the emotions.   In the setting, in the many-colored tints, in the playing of lights and shadows, the poet shows himself a perfect artist.   There are two pictures of Vivian in the full-blown splendor of her seduction, that adhere to the memory; one an open-air sketch, the other an interior scene, which vie with each other in delicacy and beauty.   The first is a symphony in green,

> He saw at first a bit of living green
> That might have been a part of all the green
> Around the tinkling fountain—

The other is a symphony in olive and crimson.   Vivian's dress, her complexion, her mass of hair, are not only made the elements of a splendid picture, but are transformed by the imagination of the poet into a floating cloud of beauty.

> The lady Vivian in a fragile sheath
> Of crimson, dimmed and veiled ineffably
> By the flame-shaken gloom wherein she sat,
> And twinkled if she moved, heard Merlin coming,
> . . . "More like a flower

Tonight," he said . . . It seemed
A flower of wonder with a crimson stem
Came leaning slowly and regretfully
To meet his will—a flower of change and peril
That had a clinging blossom of warm olive
Half-stifled with a tyranny of black,
And held the wayward fragrance of a rose
Made woman by delirious alchemy.

Such a gossamer fabric of airy splendor baffles analysis. I will not commit the indiscretion of applying the critic's knife to its throbbing life. Yet one mode of the creative process ought to be noted. It consists in the transposition from one plane of beauty to another, from the material to the immaterial, by picking among the significant features of beautiful things or startling experiences the attribute, or shade, or quality susceptible of being raised by the transmuting power of the imagination from the realm of facts to the realm of values, and expanded and broadened there until it reaches the dazzling fringe of the perfect or seems to dart into the unfathomable. This is the very essence of poetry and the supreme achievement of the poetic imagination.

This dainty and musical prelude introduces a drama of disappointment and failure. Over this graceful scene à la Botticelli hovers the dark-winged angel of destiny, whose portentous shadow reminds us that grief is the wages of folly. Merlin's love—the folly of his old age—cannot be crowned with happiness, any more than Arthur's love—the folly of his kingly caprice—or

83

Lancelot's love—the folly of his passionate rashness. The drama that is to follow grows in an atmosphere of symbols.

It is through symbolic figuration that Robinson's poetry attains its greatest power of suggestion. Through symbols it clothes human emotions in a light that throbs with subtle thought-vibrations. Through symbols it loads intellectual values with a wealth of concrete beauty. Through symbols, it reveals the mysterious correspondence of the rhythm of the universe with the rhythm of our souls, and throws us, as if on the sudden disclosure of the spirit-world, into wondering ecstasy. The *Merlin* is a poem particularly rich in symbols. There is one, so impressive by its perfect union with the most pathetic episode, that one must dwell on it a moment.

In the bower of bliss where Merlin and Vivian are enjoying the first rapture of their mutual passion, a whiff of misgiving, after some time, is felt surreptitiously to creep up and steal on the lover's felicity. How can it be otherwise? Is it possible for this ill-matched affection to last unthwarted? Will not Time wear out the hectic flame, precipitate the logic of facts, and prevail at length over an unnatural delusion? The trivial vicissitudes, which are the common ingredients of such a situation, are transmuted by the poet into symbolical beauty.

Vivian offers to Merlin a precious cup of wine from the last flagon of a rare vintage, that her "father gave to kings alone, and far from always." She presses him to drink it with her. It signifies their detachment from everything but their present happiness, or, as the poet puts it, "their victory over Time."

> Take the rest,
> That I may see tonight the end of it.
> I'll have no living remnant of the dead
> Annoying me until it fades and sours
> Of too long cherishing; for Time enjoys
> The look that's on our faces when we scowl
> On unexpected ruins.

Noticing a moment of hesitation on Merlin's part, she adds in the casual manner of a hostess:

> At the end
> Of this incomparable flowing gold
> . . . I fear there may be specks.

What was for her a meaningless remark takes on a deep significance for Merlin, whose mind is already laboring under a prescience of what is to come. Those "specks," in his reflective melancholy mood, become the symbol of the gloom gathering over their heads. The poet, with sure grasp of the mysterious bonds that relate material to spiritual things, weaves those specks into a dark thread thrust athwart the texture of their golden dream. With true philosophical insight, he connects it with the oncoming victory of Time, itself the fore-runner of Fate. Thus a spiritual drama interlinks it-self with the love-song and enlarges it. Henceforth, while the love-dalliance goes on, we never lose sight of

the impending doom. Even when Vivian, half-con-
scious of her lover's apprehensions, tries to drive away
his dark broodings, she reverts unwittingly to the
ominous shadow of Time. She endeavors to laugh it
out of their ken:

> Time's way with you and me
> Is our way, in that we are out of Time
> And out of tune with Time.

But not so for Merlin. He has already resolved to
comply with Arthur's request to sail back to Camelot.
The mist of estrangement that floats between them
thickens. He feels that the threat hovering over Arthur's kingdom is aimed at him also, who, in a different way from the King, but no less glaringly, has
swerved from the path of wisdom. Time and Fate, the
two companion-deities that hold in their hands men's
destinies, now haunt his consciousness:

> Whatever you or I may choose to name it,
> The name of it is Fate, who played with me
> And gave me eyes to read of the unwritten
> More lines than I have read.

Fate does not deal direct blows, but it sends agents who
do their appointed task relentlessly. Merlin feels he
is in the clutch of one of these emissaries. Again and
again he catches a glimpse of a warning angel, whatever Vivian does to allay his fear and coax him back
to their old carelessness:

But now he knew that his cold angel's name
Was Change, and that a mightier will than his
Or Vivian's had ordained that he be there.

Change, Time and Fate pursue the lovers, while they
vainly attempt to deceive themselves. Merlin knows
that this tri-unity of gods wields the moral and intellectual forces away from which there is no escape. And
now the "specks," which had darkened the pure trans-
parency of the golden cup, dance an ominous dance before their eyes. Vivian identifies the "specks" with all
that menaces their happiness; she sees them gathering
into a vision of a crumbling city amid flaming clouds,
which presages the fall of Camelot.

Pray take your kings and sins away somewhere
And bury them, and bury the Queen in also.
I know this king . . . There are specks
Almost all over him. Long live the king,
But not the king who lives in Camelot
With Modred, Lancelot, and Guinevere—
And all four speckled like a merry nest
Of addled eggs together.

The bitter humor of her speech conveys more clearly
than lamentations her growing consciousness of some
terrible mishap foreshadowed by the "specks." As for
Merlin, he realizes that Fate has overcome him and that
there is no resisting its dread behest.

For I am old. I was young yesterday.
Time's hand that I have held away so long
Grips hard now on my shoulder. Time has won.

The conclusion of the epic rises to a culminating height of thought where a vision of the ideal shines amid the last flickering of the soul-struggle and bathes its anguish in philosophical repose. Merlin's insight, piercing beyond distressing appearances, perceives

> In each bewildered man who dots the earth
> A moment with his days a groping thought
> Of an eternal will.

The drama, toward the end, becomes almost a pure drama of ideas. The two characters that remain on the stage, Merlin and Dagonet, exchange their reflections or rather think aloud in meditative contemplation. In spite of his sufferings at the hands of love, Merlin keeps his faith in love—in pure love, that, handing on from woman to man the enthusiasm for what transcends Self, prepares the way for great sacrifices and noble achievements. In this, Robinson follows Shelley. Like Shelley he links together love and the aspiration to the ideal. But he has been taught by the failure of the romanticists to tame love's fervor. He is not the man to call up a vision of airy nothings and feed on beauty and perfection till actual living becomes an inconsistent dream. He knows man's limitations. He makes allowance for human weaknesses and the powerlessness of mortal beings to reach the absolute. He is too keen an analyst, too clear-sighted an observer, and too much of a dramatist, to try the futile feat of floating between earth and heaven in the "intense inane." His characters are real men; he shows them torn by actual griefs, that proceed from traceable causes. But he raises the human drama of emotional and mental conflicts to the plane of the permanent and the eternal by permeating it with spiritual vision. His cult of the ideal redeems the baseness of much in life that is ungenerous or ignoble. Out of the fall of heroes and the ruin of empires, he sees a ray of light arise, that may guide future generations to a wiser husbanding of man's permitted share of happiness.

> Now Arthur, Modred, Lancelot, and Gawaine
> Are swollen thoughts of this eternal will
> Which have no other way to find the way
> That leads them on to their inheritance
> Than by the time-infuriating flame
> Of a wrecked empire, lighted by the torch
> Of woman, who, together with the light
> That Galahad found, is yet to light the world.

The *Lancelot* is a poem at once of more limited scope and of greater elaboration in the details. One may find fault with it for a certain dragging lengthiness in some places, but the poem for the most part commends itself by its penetrating and tragic expression of the eternal truths of the human heart. Love, as presented in the poem, is not the courteous edulcorated feeling of Tennyson's Knight, when he sighs his adoration on his knees within the vine-clad oriel, or the trembling torment of the same when, away from his paramour, he consumes himself with remorse. In Robinson's Lancelot, compunction, of a sort, arises only when his passion

89

begins to wane. His love, in its heyday, partakes too much of the nature of a fierce impulse, to be shaken by Victorian qualms. As a true soldier, he feels his heart equally fired by love of fighting and love of woman. As a noble human being, he is also deeply sensitive to the ideal. There is no contradiction between his passion for the Queen and his loyalty to the spirit of chivalry; for it is his passion that feeds his exalted dream, as long as it retains its freshness and force; and, when its impetus slackens, it is through worship of chivalrous loyalty and integrity that he braces himself against what he considers now as a consuming, unduly engrossing passion.

He would not be a man—in contradistinction to the lay figure of the *Idylls*—if he was not subject to the inexorable law of mutability. Instead of romantic idealization we have psychological observation and a drama of flesh and blood.

Robinson's Lancelot is no pastoral swain in armor, but a man of experience and responsibility, who gives himself up to love with his whole soul, in the season of love, and knows that a moment comes when love must break its own coils and let the soul free for further self-realization. The impetuous Knight is portrayed at the significant turning of his life, when the wear and tear of years and adverse circumstances have begun to alter him from what he was. The emphasis is laid on the inner conflicts and struggles that arise from this change. The crux lies in the clash of souls that takes place in Joyous Gard after the flight of the two lovers and after the King has come with an army to lay siege around their place of refuge. Battles are fought every day with the usual havoc of youthful lives. The rainy season has set in. We feel that dark events are brewing. There is a slackness in Lancelot's attentions to Guinevere which cannot pass unnoticed:

> He led her slowly on with a cold show
> Of care that was less heartening for the Queen
> Than anger would have been.

How is it that Lancelot's passion is abating? Is it because of sorrow for the death of dear comrades killed in his own battles? Is it reluctance to fight against the King and his own former fellow-Knights? Certainly, these are among the causes of his darkening mood. But there is a central reason that takes precedence over all the others; Lancelot's love has come to a point where it cannot last without destroying itself. Human bliss is fragile: particularly exposed to vicissitudes is the joy born from a wild unlawful love. It is one of those feverish passions that cannot be of long duration. They quicken the course of the blood and heighten the price of life, for a time. But they devour their own substance. Outward circumstances conspire against them to bring to a swifter close their natural decline. The sum of it all is contained in Lancelot's remark, sharp as steel and cold as ice: "All hours have an end."

A man like Lancelot cannot easily bear the trammels of an all-absorbing passion when its glow is passed. He has loyalties and ambitions, longings and aspirations which he must satisfy. Love was for him a stage on the road that leads to higher fulfillments. He will not be one of those

> Who feed themselves on hopes dryer than hay,
> Enjoying not what they eat, yet always eating.

He must meet his destiny, which calls him to wage more battles as a step towards greater power, and think larger thoughts as a means of approaching nearer to the Light. He will keep the memory of all that his love for Guinevere meant as an ardent and beautiful phase of his existence, hoping that she, on her side, will remain faithful to their common vision of splendor.

> And if you bid your memory now to blot
> Your story from the book of what has been,
> Your phantom happiness were a ghost indeed,
> And I the least of weasels among men,—
> Too false to manhood and your sacrifice
> To merit a niche in hell.

But when the fatal hour of parting rings, it is the man's part to speak the firm language of reason. When things have come to such an entanglement that prolonging the liaison would entail insupportable stress and bring ruin to both, it is for the man to stiffen in the attitude commanded by the inevitable. The woman will cling to the shadow of the past with desperate hope against all hope. On this opposition of the masculine and feminine psychology rests the dramatic climax of the poem. In passage after passage cries of entreaty or

reproach, humble submission or weak revolt, pressing
endearment or galling anger, issue from Guinevere's
mouth, in pathetic helplessness.　She pleads pitifully:

> 　　　　　　　　　　　　If our world—
> Your world and mine and Arthur's, as you say—
> Is going out now to make way for another,
> Why not before it goes, and I go with it,
> Have yet one morsel more of life together,
> Before death sweeps the table and our few crumbs
> Of love are a few last ashes? . . .

She moans in miserable retrospect:

> 　　　　　　　　　Is there nothing left of me?
> Nothing of what you called your white and gold,
> And made so much of? . . .　Have I lost myself
> So fast that what a mirror says I am
> Is not what is, but only what was once?
> Does half a year do that with us?

Such pangs of grief are the pathetic expression of
human truth.　They voice feminine passion in its irresponsible onset.　Beyond this, sorrow overreaches itself and calms down to a dull pain, closely resembling
resignation.　Guinevere falls into a state of detachment from all that she accounted dear and precious, and
finally resolves to take refuge at the convent of Almesbury.　There is a last meeting of the lovers between the
four cold walls of the monastery.　It is her turn now
to remain impassive, in her death-like unconcern for
all life's interests.　His it is to experience a momentary

acute revival of the old love, in a whirl of retrospective passion when the whole past suddenly flashes back with an intense gleam of burning anguish. The contrast of the mind's vision and the pitiable reality is of powerful tragic effect. She, who has consummated the supreme sacrifice, has the advantage over him, who remaining of this world, identifies himself with the man he used to be and feels the sharp bite of regret. She reminds him of his own words, at the former cruel parting:

> Was it you,
> Or was it Gawaine who said once to me,
> "We cannot make one world of two, nor may we
> Count one life more than one. Could we go back
> To the old garden, we should not stay long!"

The words pierce through him as daggers, just as they had stabbed her heart when he had pronounced them. A moment after, she joins the sisters who are marching to chapel two by two with clasped hands and bent heads. A chill bewilderment seizes Lancelot:

> In one long wave it whelmed him, and then broke—
> Leaving him like a lone man on a reef,
> Staring for what had been with him, but now
> Was gone and was a white face under the sea,
> Alive there, and alone—always alone.

Concrete beauty enhances psychological truth, both blended into dramatic unity by the constructive power of the imagination. Beauty is everywhere, in the *Lancelot* as well as in the *Merlin*. We must not leave

94

the poems without presenting a few remarks on their
qualities of form, which contribute powerfully to give
them their high rank among the great Arthurian epics.

The metaphors are often striking for their ingenious
originality. When Merlin reproaches Vivian with
brooding too much on the "specks" he says:

> Why does a woman,
> Made otherwise a miracle of love
> And loveliness, and of immortal beauty,
> Tear one word by the roots out of a thousand,
> And worry it, and torture it, and shake it,
> Like a small dog that has a rag to play with?

Two images, one perceived by the eyes, the other arising from the imagination often blend into harmonious
richness—as when Vivian, dressed for the evening feast,
is awaiting Merlin, in the semi-darkness of her boudoir:

> . . . she knew and felt the slower tread
> Of his unseen advance among the shadows,
> To the small haven of uncertain light
> That held her in it *as a torch-lit shoal*
> *Might hold a smooth red fish* . . .

One vivid simile sometimes gives the thought poignant immediacy:

> The King, who sat with folded arms, now bowed
> His head and felt, *unfought and all aflame*
> *Like immanent hell-fire,* the wretchedness
> That only those who are to lead may feel . . .

95

Or the fullness of concrete beauty is contained in one epithet, so chosen as to project the melancholy mellowness of the twilight hour on a mood, as when the King says:

> I get *gray* comfort of dark words.

Or, conversely, this sharp intensity of a mood throws over nature an impalpable haze of intellectual vibration. Arthur is haunted in his sleep by visions,

> Born horribly of memories and new fears
> That, *in the gray-lit irony of dawn,*
> Were partly to fade out and be forgotten.

The poet, more than once, is a painter who plies the brush like a master of the interplay of lights and shadows. Vivian sat,

> Between two shining silver candlesticks
> That lifted each a trembling flame to make
> The rest of her a dusky loveliness
> Against a bank of shadow . . .

A single line can be turned into a plastic vision:

> . . . (she) yoked his willing neck
> With half her weight.

As a princely palace decorated with precious tapestries and shapely marble groups, Robinson's style abounds in brilliant and tasteful beauties. What is more, the general texture of his verse is full of charm and intellectual finish. His style is thoroughly original. It is a constant creation. Its chief characteristic is a subtle involution of thought united with a great simplicity of expression. It winds out like a delicate embroidery made of threads of finely sorted hues. One wonders how such masterly effects can be achieved with such a strict husbandry of the resources of the language. There is no resisting the winning suggestiveness of those smooth lines, so chary of verbal flourish. The exact correspondence of the words to the thought, the elastic pace, the quaint homeliness endow them with a rare elegance, the more felt as it contrasts with the supple sinuosity of the ideas and the feelings. The poet imparts pathos and conjures up wonder by apparently plain, short clauses, whose elementary power searches like the rays of a spot-light. He needs none of the rhetoric of the romantic poets to express the mystery of the immaterial. How simply, and yet irresistibly does Merlin acknowledge the nobleness of Vivian's ideal, however mixed it may be with earthly designs:

> . . . and I shall pray that all be well
> With Vivian, whose unquiet heart is hungry
> For what is not, and what shall never be
> Without her, in a world that men are making,
> Knowing not how, nor caring yet to know . . .
> Though Vivian, in her golden shell of exile,
> Knows now and cares, not knowing that she cares,
> Nor caring that she knows.

Romance and pathos float through the transparent unsophisticated vocabulary of Merlin's speech, where he intimates the uncertainty of man's prestige, even when he who tries to conjure the secret of the future is a prophet and a seer:

> The man who sees
> May see too far, and he may see too late
> The path he takes unseen . . .

Such thrifty musical directness is a triumph of refinement.

The *Tristram,* which was published seven years after *Lancelot,* deserves, for its stately structure, its dramatic force and its finish of expression, to be considered as the principal and commanding part of the trilogy on the Arthurian legend. Robinson's constructive genius must have conceived the organic plan of the tripartite epic before he began to work out the separate episodes, so well each fits in with the others, so proportionately each contributes to the total beauty. In the last capital composition, complete in itself, linked to the companion-poems by a few threads of the plot and by the general tone and atmosphere, the author fused into supreme harmony the serenity that floats in the wake of a bygone age and the present unrest of self-analysing souls, aware of the sadness which retrospect and foresight throw like a shadow over men's most cherished desires.

We hail the poem as Robinson's masterpiece by reason of its storm-assaulted olympian majesty, pure in outline, complex in substance, remarkably free from some defects which the author had not quite succeeded in avoiding before, rich in beauties which spring from the fruitful alliance of inspiration with consummate art, objective in its conception, yet instinct with the personality of the maker in its strength and winsomeness.

The defect of occasional obscurity has disappeared, as if the splendor of the theme and the consequent glow of the poet's imagination had caused light to enter into the passages of densest meaning. Through his insight into the workings of the mind and heart, owing to his sense of the hidden relations between the life of the soul and the life of nature, by dint of skill in the architectonics, and thanks to sureness and precision in the wording of the lines and the building of the periods, Robinson has well-nigh succeeded in keeping perfect balance between intellect and feeling and perfect correspondence between thought and expression. He sacrificed none of the speculative complexities which he knows how to extract from the characters and the situations; but he projected into them rays of brightness that seem to flow purer from a mind ripened by experience and reflection.

Are there no blemishes? Some parts, such as the IVth, Vth, and VIth, may be found at times overburdened with details and long-drawn-out. I do not deny that staunch admirers of Robinson's artistry have a right to contend there is charm even in those pages less firmly supported by the swiftness of the action or the warmth of life. Exacting readers, on the other hand, may criticize such or such secondary figure because it is given too much importance, such or such particular because it duplicates another that came before, such or such development because in it the interest flags. Perchance we are made aware of certain infrequent weaknesses mostly by contrast with the great passages, which are always distinguished by exceptional and exquisite beauty.

Other faultfinders there may be who reproach the poet with not conforming to the lineaments of the mediaeval story. Yet in this he only claimed the freedom which the old authors of metrical romances and their continuator, Thomas Malory, made use of. Even a hasty glance at the diluted and wearisome version handed down to us in the *Morte d'Arthur* will show the unmistakable superiority of the modern poet. The changes he introduced are of an observer of psychological facts, a master of dramatic effects, and an artist. He overreaches the old jongleurs by all that thought and art have gained in the course of seven centuries; and he surpasses his nearer predecessors, Swinburne and Matthew Arnold, by the undeniably greater power, finesse and variety of his inspiration.

True to the design already adopted in his other Arthurian epics, he does away with the marvellous, which would be out of place in a poem based upon psychological truth, where the episodes are carefully sifted in order to bring out significantly human conflicts and thought-inspiring vicissitudes of the soul. In this he asserts his determination to link the lyricism of love to actual observation, and to construct the tragedy on conscious

100

esthetics, which substitute concentration for dispersion. He preserves the salient features of the old tale, the local coloring, the heroic grandeur, the romantic remoteness, especially the pathetic love-motive, impersonated in the legendary hero and heroine, and the poignant atmosphere of sadness flecked with fleeting flashes of joy. He voices that passion in unforgetable accents, through novel, splendid images, with a great richness of emotion, in a style ordered with a classic sense of the economy of means. But he leaves aside the myth of the love-philter; he strikes off the merely fabulous incidents; and he changes the dénouement.

Many a reader will experience a sort of *a priori* regret not to find at the end Tristram's anxious waiting for the ship, which, with its white or black sail, is to bring him life or death. But, after perusing the close of the love-episode in Robinson's poem, he will feel so deeply for the two unfortunates mowed down at one fateful blow, in the acme of passion, that he will readily grant the poet's right to conclude in his own way his original rendering of the story. He will realize that the catastrophe, with so much of the pathos of the Greek drama about it, adds an element of relentless inevitability, more provocative of terror and pity than the betrayal of the hero by the false Isolt of Brittany.

Freed from superannuated witchcraft, cleared from adventitious arabesques, the story is fit to be handled by a master of psychological observation. The characters are given distinctive mental features—which in no way detracts from their symbolic value, while uncovering in them depths of human signification. They appeal to the mind as well as to the heart. Not that the intellectual element is ever crammed in so as to interfere with the naturalness of the dialogue or to slacken the movement of the narrative. The inner portraiture comes out through light touches; it expresses itself in acts and attitudes; it permeates the speeches; it brings about oppositions of characters or variations of tone, while the main theme of imperious passion unfolds itself, as delicately shaded as powerfully unified. The poet eschews the pitfall of too much analysis. It is the regrets, the fears, the hopes, the cruel surprises, the snatches of happiness—the passion with its exultation or despondency, its fond illusions or sharp encounters with the asperities of life—that form the woof and warp of that tragedy of two burning souls. Analysis plays its part in the shaping of the characters, without being unduly pushed to the front. Through a harmonious dosage of intellectuality and sensibility, the poet preserves the traditional beauty of the subject, while enriching and renewing its intimate texture and adapting it to the modern spirit.

The composition is a model of the classic power of grasp and of rational ordering. The two great love scenes between Tristram and Isolt of Ireland—the supremely beautiful and tragic core of the poem—are incased in a prelude and a postlude, which bring in Isolt of Brittany, first as a girl, plaintively lamenting Tristram's departure, then as a wife, hearing of Tristram's death and plaintively mourning for his fate and hers.

Thus framed in, the love drama takes place, at Tintagel, then at Joyous Gard, divided in the middle by Tristram's time of exile, during which he is induced by grief and pity to contract a marriage, which he will never consider as a binding union. The prelude makes us acquainted with the characters and their doings previous to the opening of the story; it serves as a preparation for the tragic events that are to follow, by creating an atmosphere of wistful expectation. The middle episode provides, as it were, a resting place, where we collect ourselves after the strain of the first act. In the postlude, we survey from a point of vantage the havoc worked by fate and death, and gradually come back to a state of comparative composure, where we give ourselves up to the spell of the becalmed melody and to the catharsis of pity and sorrow.

The excellence of the poem lies chiefly in the picture of the uncontrollable, danger-fraught, fond passion which throws into each other's arms Tristram and Isolt, who cannot be united by the bonds of a lawful union. The poet's divining of the secrets of the heart, his lyrical genius and his power of dramatic emotion give him a high rank among the initiates of Apollo's mysteries. Concrete beauty—the setting of gorgeous nature, the entrancing loveliness of human faces, the winning spontaneity or awful stateliness of attitudes—accompanies the description of the feelings and makes it instant and real. The thrilling combination of sensuousness and spirituality appears in the very opening lines, when Isolt, but dimly visible in the pale moonlight, slowly

descends the grand staircase from the castle to meet
Tristram.

> Isolt of Ireland,
> With all her dark young majesty unshaken
> By grief and shame and fear that made her shake
> Till to go further would have been to fall,
> Came nearer still to him and still said nothing,
> Till terror born of passion became passion
> Reborn of terror while his lips and hers
> Put speech out like a flame put out by fire.

The intensity of the lyrical love-duet is already contained in this plastic and pathetic passage, where repeated words sing like the notes of a musical phrase in
a powerful crescendo. The lovers silently listen to the
beating of their hearts, ready to leap out in the infinite,
were they not chained down by the fetters of anguish.
It is Isolt that breaks the coil of paralysing terror. How
true to life! For it is she whose young soul, throbbing
with desire, was bruised by the conjuration of an indifferent father and a hated husband. Her wild escape—
for a moment—towards the freedom of true love is
goaded on by revolt. There is a dash of defiance in
her passionate rashness, curbed hitherto by her maidenly pride and obedience to formal law. Her love has
suddenly acquired the strength which accrues to fiery
souls from excess of indignity.

Gradually, her words and acts reveal the inner
vehemence. Tristram but reluctantly yields to the impulse of his own heart, still vaguely kept back by chivalrous allegiance to his liege-lord, above all knowing that

any imprudent move, doomed by fate to failure, may ruin her whom he cherishes above his own life. The dialogue which takes place is rich in dramatic implications. It is no mere outflow of lyrical sweetness and pathos, such as a poet with a gift of virtuosity might devise and sustain with clever developments. It is an exchange of thoughts pulsing with passion and of passionate utterances loaded with thoughts—thoughts called by a retrospect of the past, reflections on the present, misgivings about the future, insight into truths of universal import, intimations of the great mystery which surrounds our insecure life—all commanded by the necessity of the case and the logic of the sensibility and the imagination.

The poet has associated love with death and fate, calling up the mighty antithesis which all great lyrists have sensed to be the most moving of dramatic themes. Murderous revenge on the part of a jealous villain will come only at the end. At the outset, Tristram is haunted by a gloomy yearning after self-inflicted death, under the unbearable stress of grief. Isolt shrinks before the racking anticipation of death-in-life, in the loathsome embrace of King Mark. Both lovers pale at the thought of the inevitable separation, which means death for their souls. The shadow of fate passes over their minds; for they realize all that there was of preordained necessity in their former silence and in the present resistless upwelling of their innermost being. In the midst of blissful ecstasy, they shudder at the unfathomableness of the future.

Isolt is the one who, in an outburst of bravery, signifies her will not to let the past prey upon the fleeting moments of their reunion, or dark apprehensions ruin what there may remain for them of promise.

> Are you sure that a word given
> Is always worth more than a world forsaken?

She insists that some favorable circumstances may supervene to liberate them from their dire necessity:

> Tristram, fair things yet
> Will have a shadow black as night before them,
> And soon will have a shadow black as night
> Behind them.   And all this may be a shadow,
> Sometime, that we may live to see behind us—
> Wishing that we had not been all so sure
> Tonight that it was always to be night.

It is she who looks fate in the face, and speaks words of hope, and "muffles his mouth with kisses," when he offers to yield to despair.   He, for all his passion, cannot silence his intellect, which will look backward and forward, linking self-censure with regret, weighing remote consequences, pleading the bitter restraint of prudence.   He has enough self-control to scan his own recent doings and pass biting criticism upon his unwitting indiscretion.   Alluding to his fight with Isolt's cousin, Morhaus, the wicked giant, he says:

> When a man sues
> The fairest of all women for her love,
> He does not cleave the skull first of her kinsman
> To mark himself a man.   That was my way . . .

106

—a piece of sarcasm which recalls the lashes of irony the heroes of the ancient Greek drama often inflict upon themselves, as the last rebuff of man in his unequal struggle against fate.

Tristram indulges in melancholy reflections, like one who, defeated by adverse circumstances, rises superior to their blind tyranny by the noble exercise of consciousness and reason. Time, he remarks, has a double face: now he frowns on love and threatens it with destruction; now he smiles on love and opens to it a vista on the future. God has a double face: for there is the God that rebukes wild love and threatens retribution to fond lovers; and there is the God that decrees love and appoints the hour when lovers are to meet. Sin has a double face: for there is the sin according to the unjust code of conventional morality, which makes it a crime for innocent ones to love each other; and there is the sin committed by God himself (as independent spirits dare proclaim), when He created love, and did not grant it freedom.

The wistfulness that pervades the scene is in keeping with the traditional features of the Celtic soul, and admits of streaks of passion and rays of intellectual light in keeping with the modern state of mind. The poet sympathizes with the spirit of revery that hovers about the towers of Tintagel, the thickets of the Forest Perilous and the peaks of Morven, evincing at the same time a firm grasp of the spiritual beauty which has grown in our reflective age out of the consciousness of human frailty and grandeur. He does it with ease and

107

with a sincerity of feeling as far from the languor of mawkish sentiment as from the false glitter of romantic finery. His proper qualities are naturalness and truth, allied to dramatic force, lyrical glamour and suggestive thoughtfulness. He reconciles depth with simplicity. The every-day vocabulary often suffices him to express the most intense feelings. The magic lies in the choice and order of words, in the rhythms, in the repetitions which now mark the incessant recurrence of haunting feelings, now follow the circuitous movements of the thought round the axis of passion. The returns of the same means of expression translate the pulses of the soul under the stress of engrossing motives or dominating ideas. In this elaborately simplified style, there is a delicacy of artistic perception, a purity of outline, a harmony of utterance, which send through the verse, without effort, the thrill of great poetry.

> Tristram, believe
> That if I die my love will not be dead,
> As I believe that yours will not be dead.
> If in some after time your will may be
> To slay it for the sake of a new face,
> It will not die. Whatever you do to it,
> It will not die. We cannot make it die,
> We are not mighty enough to sentence love
> Stronger than death to die, though we may die.

. Time is conquered; death is defeated; fate weakens. The superhuman love of these human lovers soars in the empyrean, where it will find its proper environment, infinite space and eternal duration. Nature, overthrowing the barriers where she seemed to be penned in, wings her flight to the sphere of the ideal—for a moment! For fear steals back, too well justified by the dangers that lie in wait on all sides—at the gates of the castle where sentinels are posted; in the palace where Queen Morgan (who covets Tristram for herself) is on the lookout; in the heart of King Mark whose jealousy is getting awakened; there in the garden where Andred the traitor is prowling.

Tristram avoids death, but he is condemned to take the road of exile.

When, after many months, the two lovers meet again, it is at Joyous Gard, on Lancelot's estate, in eastern Britain. Mark is in prison, by King Arthur's order, for some transgression to the laws of chivalry. It is no short or precarious interview, this time, but a lasting and seemingly secure reunion . . . as human things go. Isolt has lost her bravery. Sick with humiliation, broken down by long waiting, cowed down by some superstitious fear that Mark's revenge may still reach them, it is her turn to tremble on the threshold of Paradise regained. Tristram, on the contrary, feels himself freed from all obligations, since Mark, by driving him away, has become his declared enemy. His passion cannot be greater than it was, but it is braced now by a strength of resolution which his will had not known before. This reversal of parts wears the double beauty of being conformable to the natural evolution of the characters and of introducing a novelty of accent in a situation not unlike the former, where a writer less versed in the knowledge of the human heart might have let some monotony slip in.

In the first love scene, the author had depicted ardent passion unconsummated. Now all indicates that the ideal flame of two souls has become the fiery ardor of two beings of flesh and blood. Robinson resorts to indirection and suggestion—within the limits of his wonted reserve—to depict a situation where the modern school of the sex-appeal would seize on every opportunity to pile up crudities. The elevated tone corresponds to the strict decorum of the attitudes. Tristram's heightened spirits express themselves in lyrical strains, occasionally interrupted by that subtle exercise of the intellect, by which a man under the power of a strong sentiment avers himself in complete possession of his reason. In a similar case, in the first act, the result was irony or grim humor; here it is pleasantry or cheerful humor. Isolt again "muffles his mouth with kisses," but not for the same motive as before. There it was because Tristram, in words which she deemed inauspicious, expressed discouragement and fear. Here it is because Tristram, in words which she deems dangerous, expresses contentment and joy. The parallelism of the two reversed situations brings out the change which has taken place in the characters, emphasizing at the same time the permanence of their deeper feelings. What would appear artificial, were the situations forced, turns out a felicitous treatment, because it conforms to human truth.

At times, Tristram makes his hopefulness almost infectious; at times, he half falls under the influence of Isolt's despondency. Thus the dialogue passes through alternations of buoyancy and depression. At length, valiance takes the upper hand. . . . Isolt yields to the irresistible efflux that emanates from the hero's courageous trust. Holding her in close embrace, he murmurs to her ear:

> Never believe—never believe again—
> Your fear for me was more than love. Time lied,
> If he said that. When we are done with time,
> There is no time for fear. It was not fear—
> It was love's other name. Say it was that!
> Say to me it was only one of time's lies!
> Whatever it was—never mind what it was!
> There will be time enough for me to die.
> Never mind death tonight . . . Isolt! Isolt!

It is a short period of bliss. Jealous Mark and murderous Andred return: it means death for the two lovers.

The passages which we have quoted have shown that, with Robinson, expression and conception are on a par. We must insist on the form of the poem, because the externals, here, are intimately related to the contents.

The poet's imagination is characterized now by amplitude—with the effect of extending the vision into the immaterial and the infinite; now by vigor—with the effect of concentrating ideas or feelings into a vivid sensation. The former quality often depends on the

111

opportune use of abstractions. Robinson does it with pertinency and justness. It cannot be said of him, as of not a few symbolists, that he courts impreciseness. If at times the universe seems to dissolve before the eyes of his heroes, it is because he feels that their inner disturbance puts them, at moments of anguish or of ecstasy, out of touch with what gives to the material world its substantiality.

A few examples of the use of abstractions will illustrate the part they play in creating an atmosphere of ideality. When Tristram was alone in the dark, on the terrace of Tintagel gardens,

> Gazing at emptiness for a long time,
> He looked away from life. . . .

Tristram, by the side of Isolt of Brittany, felt

> Within her candor and her artlessness
> The still white fire of her necessity.

How mysteriously rises the figure of Isolt of Ireland, with her pride, her beauty and her fiery nature,—Isolt

> Of the patrician passionate helplessness!

Sensuous elements timely brought in give a concrete value to impressions that might remain frigid or vague. A sentiment, when associated once with a rich sensation, becomes inseparably linked to it, recurring like a poetical burden where descriptive color mixes with lyrical intensity. Of this nature is the melancholy moan of

the Cornish waves on the Cornish rocks, which forms
the bass accompaniment to the love duet at Tintagel,
and resounds in the lovers' memory whenever they get
snatches of the old bliss, overshadowed by the same
threatening omens. In like manner, the incessant flight
of the sea-gulls, watched by Isolt of Brittany from the
shore, returns in the poem, like their own circle over
the ocean, to symbolize the eternal waiting of the disappointed bride, ever looking towards the west, ever in
vain.

Images shape themselves in the poet's mind—colored
landscapes, shadowy visions, chiaroscuro pictures, brief
animated scenes, attitudes caught at a glance—which
form a frame, a background, an illustration, for the most
striking passages, or transfer to the plane of the visible
and the tangible the elements that belong to the intellect
or the sensibility.

Now it is a fresco half realistic, half visionary:

> A forest-hidden sunset filled long clouds
> Eastward over the sea with a last fire,
> Dim fire far off, wherein Tristram beheld
> Tintagel slowly smouldering in the west
> To a last darkness. . . .

Now it is a painted scene with tragic contrasts, in the
manner of Goya, as when Tristram, coming back from
the forest with an armful of flowers, learns that Isolt
has been carried away by King Mark's attendants:

> Tristram
> Dropped like a log; and silent on the floor,

113

With wild flowers lying around him on the floor—
Wild roses for Isolt—lay like a log.

Now a play of light and shadow brings into dim relief
a half blurred figure (Queen Morgan):

> Tristram saw
> Before him a white neck and a white bosom
> Beneath a fair and feline face whereon
> Demure determination was engraved
> As on a piece of moonlit living marble.

The poet does not even need to pen a description, or
limn a portrait, or introduce a metaphor to call up the
image which crystallizes in his mind. One word is
enough. His originality and force reveal themselves in
his choice of epithets. They have novelty, unexpectedness, power of suggestion, plenitude and a swift flashing
splendor.

A moment of rest after the strain of passion:

> Release from such a fettered ecstasy.

Tristram, angry with himself for his dullness, deplores

> How little of his blind self a crowded youth,
> With a sight error-flecked and pleasure-flawed,
> Had made him see.

Sentenced to exile, he flees in the rain,

> Along a road that had no sodden end.

By the side of Isolt of Brittany, he yields out of commiseration,

114

To her gray eyes and her white need of him.

He thinks of the other Isolt, in her western loneliness:

Isolt of the wild frightened violet eyes . . .
Beyond those endless evening leagues.

Sometimes the effect of concentration, depth or ideality lies in the alliance of the epithet with the noun, evocative of so much significance and mysterious beauty, that we cannot but dwell to wonder:

All her firm litheness melted
Into the sure surrender of a child.

Dimly deceived
By the dark surety of her stateliness
And by the dark indignity of distance. . . .

. . . till he was saying
Muffled and husky words that groped and faltered,
Half silenced in a darkness of warm hair.

Although the sifting and the coupling of words may seem sometimes rather elaborate, it wears the mark of such fine sensitiveness and intellectuality, in so close accord with the situation and feelings, that the reader is compelled to assent. Robinson's art, with all its subtlety, is ingenuous. He does not seek the rare; his manner is rare, because the keenness of his observation, the sagacity of his judgment, the promptness of his sensibility make it inevitably so. He could not possess that delicate charm, that catching sweetness, that winsome grace—which no analysis can account for, because it is impalpable as life—were he not natural.

That remark holds good for his style at large. Its outstanding feature is the union of fine perception with reasonableness. The head keeps active when the heart is astir. He is not the poet of stormy passion. He does not stress his genius to vie with the simoon. There are enough adepts of frenzied literature without him. His it is to defend the rights of meditative and poised poetry. His gift of intellectual analysis does not detract from his sense of beauty or from his sympathy for men's joys and sorrows. This dualism explains his well-balanced view of the things of the heart and of the mind, and accounts for his winding ways of expression. His veracity and sincerity cannot but strike those who have taken some pains to grasp his thoughts and feelings— that is, have conversed with his work more than by chance or at random, and have willingly given themselves up to his power of suggestion. Attenuated tints predominate over glaring or dazzling strokes of the brush—except when the *vis tragica* carries all reserve away, and, without any violation of the rules of taste, there rises a cry of anguish or exultation.

Robinson resolves wholes into their component parts, traces shadings in nooks and corners, composes soulharmonies rich in overtones. Therefrom proceed the sinuous ways of his sentences and periods, the oppositions of terms that set the negative against the affirmative, the repetitions of words with slight variations of meaning. Sometimes a certain monotony steals in.

116

Generally, however, the return of the same phrase corresponds to that need of singing, as in psalms or litanies, which takes hold of the human soul at hours of excitement or of dejection.

The search of fine shadings, the respect for niceties, the portrayal of characters that do not yield to the brutal impact of passions, but listen to the voice of modesty or of noble aspiration, lead the poet to resort to indirect methods of expression. The use of the double negative, for instance, is particularly happy, when Isolt full of bravery, yet not unscared by the dangers that lurk in the dark, ventures words of hope:

> Why do you pour these frozen words
> On one who cannot be so confident
> As you that we may not be nearer life,
> Even here tonight, than we are near to death?

Sometimes the language lays siege to the thought, as it were, instead of attacking it with the bare word. This has nothing in common with the use of the periphrasis as used by the pseudo-classicists: there is a largeness and richness in the phrase which bear witness to the spontaneity of the inspiration. . . . In a close embrace the two lovers mix their breath and their looks, not needing speech to communicate what they feel:

> Each with unyielding lips refused the other
> Language unasked . . .

Sometimes a sentence, made up of a startling antithesis, looks at first sight like an enigma. Thus, Tristram, in

his sour and lonely mood on the terrace, summoned by
Mark to come back to the festive hall, sends word
through Queen Morgan:

> Say to the king I feasted overmuch . . .
> An error that apology too soon
> Might qualify too late.

Too subtle? No. For Tristram, the nimble-minded
minstrel, knows that this apology to the King at the
hour of his wrath comes too soon; but, as it is the only
moment when it can be given, it will be inopportune,
useless, like words uttered too late.

Complexity of expression is the natural counterpart
of complexity of thought. Robinson scrutinizes the
minds and fathoms the hearts. In the recesses of the
conscience, he discovers hesitations that foil desires,
doubts that undermine faith, contradictory motives that
divide the will against itself. He wants to voice all
that; for in all that lies psychological truth, which in
our reflective age ought to be the chief object of literature. The marvel is that, calling so much on the faculties of the mind, he preserves such freshness of feelings
and genuineness of emotion. These qualities are rife in
Tristram. They will secure for the poem an exalted
rank among the few works that unite dramatic force with
depth of observation; they will make it live as the sublimated expression of love and sorrow, and the picture
of human weakness raised by the magic of creative
genius above the butts of fate and the vicissitudes of
mortality.

CHAPTER IV

Interpretative and Dramatic Poetry

ALL great poetry must be an interpretation of human character and of human life. The proper object of man's study is man, whether the mode of inquiry be abstract disquisition or a concrete rendering of the inner workings of the soul through vivid description and impassioned utterance. Verse, applied to the subject of humanity, can search deeper and express more than prose, because it is dynamic as life and synthetic as emotion, and concentrates in a few heart-probing words and phrases what prose is apt to dilute in too explicit paragraphs. It rested with Robinson, who has so closely associated thought and feeling in his lyrics, to approach character-painting and dramatic narrative with a keen insight into psychological truth, without losing anything of his imaginative vision, power of emotion or grasp of outward beauty. He draws portraits that reveal the deeper aspects of men's minds or feelings with unforgetable life-likeness and precision. He describes in detail acute intellectual or emotional crises, or sketches in bold outline a whole life-course, scanning the inmost recesses of the soul and compelling the facts of the mind to yield their full content of intellectual value. He is subtle and veracious, critical and sympathetic, elusive and suggestive, and, while thrusting the whole force of his penetrating intellect into his scenes, he wraps them in a veil of mystery as befits the rendering of evanescent realities in which so much remains unexplained. A philosophical interpretation of life.arises from the drama that unrolls before our eyes, often cheerless, as proceeding from a mind that measures the abyss between the ordinary mediocrity of man and the lofty goal he might attain. Yet there spreads over this grayness such a glow of sympathy that it counteracts whatever there may lurk in it of despondency; and there is so much interested wonder, on the part of the observer, at the recurrent proofs of man's capacity to work his own misfortune, that we share in his startled surprise and melancholy.

The epithet "dramatic" describes best Robinson's meditative ramblings through human character and passions, under the provision that we delimitate the meaning of the word as required by his particular manner. He is not dramatic, as most story-tellers are, because he delineates dire conflicts of the feelings in passionate hearts, or wild oppositions of desires or ambitions in the competition for place or power, or heinous deeds that overtly or covertly drift toward crime. He is dramatic in a broader sense, as one who traces the subtler reverberation of disappointment, or frustrated aspiration, or self-misunderstanding in gentle souls, or nerveless self-indulgence in moral wretches. When he does describe a conflict of feelings, he makes its dramatic force to lie in the doubts, waverings, unconfessed expectations, frantic yearnings that agitate the troubled soul, not in facts or actions that may bring about physical ruin. The psychological drama is developed in all its possibilities; the spectacular phases of it are left in the background. When the catastrophe brings in death, it is shadowed forth in allusive hints rather than treated as a sensational element of the tale. He is as eager to avoid violent effects, as less refined writers are to appropriate them. His pathos appeals to the intellect, never to the nerves.

His analytical and interpretative manner is related to the school founded by Robert Browning in the middle of the XIXth century. Its favorite forms of concentrated narrative and dramatic monologue or dialogue were started by Browning. But the imitation stops there. The spirit and the manner of expression are Robinson's own. He has no more indebtedness to the English master than Milton to Virgil or Wordsworth to Cowper. To Browning belongs the glory of having created the literary type—although he himself owed something to Southey and Landor. Robinson moves with his own deliberate gait on the path opened by his great predecessor. He is not so much interested as Browning in historical characters or in the picturesque setting provided by the manners and events of some past era. Browning depicted characters of broad human import under the features of Syrian leech, mediaeval knight or Italian painter. Although Robinson does not refrain from occasional incursions into the annals of the past or legends that have become the common property of the world, he is generally satisfied with observing the men and women that live about him in his wood-encircled village of Maine, U. S. A. His keen observation discovers in those homely individuals a richness of psychological and emotional complexity, a wealth of moral and intellectual materials, and a variety of mental features, which show that contemporary America stands second to no age or country in elements of human interest. He raises common people who live next-door or at the corner of the street or in a neighboring farm to the dignity of universal types where we are made to see subtle moods, mental attitudes, capacities of feelings, peculiarities of conscience, which give us a wider or deeper knowledge of our own kin. He is broadly American for the background of his narratives, however succinct, suggests the New England country, and because it is mostly in America, where traditions are least operative and individualism is best favored by circumstances, that strange and original personalities like those described can fully develop. But his characters are not provincial, for his powerful insight into general truth keeps him away from the by-paths where he might saunter in pursuit of trifling banalities. His delineation has a breadth, his dramatic construction a solidity, which impart to his work a quality of classic universality, the more striking as his style is distinctly individual and wears a decidedly modern outward aspect. He is a modern classic, that is one who does not let himself be impounded in the narrow bounds of his subjectivity, however strongly he relies on subjective inspiration to

give circumstantial novelty and specific coloring to the
personal imprint he stamps on wide-reaching observation and thoughts. Robinson's narratives have the
double character of universality of conception and individuality of form. They are classic as destined to out-
live the taste of a day and pass on to posterity with an
ever-felt quality of verisimilitude and thoughtfulness.

There is a progress in his work from the simple to
the complex. He first tried his hand at character-drawing within the limits of the sonnet, as some sculptors
carve cameos or figure-heads before attacking with the
chisel a marble-block to chip from it a life-size statue.

These sonnets, published in Robinson's first volume,
offer already the outstanding characteristic that is to be
found in his later work: they set forth one prominent
trait or describe one striking situation or gesture, in
which the whole personality of a person is contained,
as the soul of the flower in its odor. Here, the strength
of the picture lies in the compactness and sharp relief
of the chief features. Later on, the same power of con-
densation, enriched by observation and thought, enables
the poet to group around one salient feature all the facts
of the mind that take from it their significance, and, as it
were, their existence. But the early sketches are already so full and so suggestive that we feel them capable
of rich psychological development.

Aaron Stark, the Shylock of Tilbury Town, is not a
mere grotesque. Through the unseemly features of
the shrivelled old man, dimly beams his ugly soul. He
relents only from his hard stare when he hears in the

voice of others a strain of commiseration for his apparent wretchedness: a contemptuous smile is then seen to flicker over his face. In *Cliff Klingenhagen*, one might interpret as a mere physical gesture the man's strange manner of pledging a friend, when he fills the friend's glass with wine and his own with wormwood: it is a symbol, from which one may learn the lesson of self-discipline. Fleming Helphenstine is one of those men whose genial smile seems to announce a generous soul and a disposition to lavish their friendship on new-comers: that friendship lasts no longer than a bonfire in midsummer. How misleading the appearance or behavior of men when we unguardedly infer from outward signs their inward nature, is a constant cause of wonder for the poet. He knows how to impart his impression to the reader by delicate touches. A word of doubt, a note of hesitation express his feeling of the impalpableness of man's deeper personality; a troubling twinge of the face, an enigmatic glance, caught by his keen eye, give him—and us—a warning that something strange may be expected. Sometimes the revelation is sudden, and the wonder turns to pathos, as in the case of Richard Cory. Favored with wealth, a handsome mien, intelligence and taste, Cory was a perfect gentleman. A certain evasiveness of manner alone prevented his friends from feeling sure that they knew him.

> So on we worked, and waited for the light,
> And went without the meat, and cursed the bread;
> And Richard Cory, one calm summer night,
> Went home and put a bullet through his head.

These early portraits contain in germ the poetical and psychological elements which Robinson was later to develop more fully. Compared to his ulterior productions, they are what the bud is to the bloom or to the ripe fruit. In the later poems, there hovers about the characters a misty quality, as of a face seen in the dusk, which suggests the mystery of man's inner nature. The play of lights and shadows and the little impressionistic touches, which the poet successfully adds to the drawing and coloring, finally cause the mental features to loom out of the semi-darkness which dims the communication of spirit with spirit. By pondering on the complexities of the soul, Robinson does not only make himself possessed of a large store of psychological knowledge, but his technique grows richer. A finer intuition furnishes him with more perfect means to express his thought. He is not content with telling in his own name the results of his sympathetic contemplation: he calls on other characters to bring in their observations. Sometimes he represents his view as conflicting with that of the fictitious observer, and from this opposition of opinions spurt vivid sparks of light. Sometimes he lets us see the characters solely through the judgments of others, whose likings, dislikes and mental dispositions, carefully described, determine their feelings and impressions and introduce a novel point of view.

Nimmo is a married man, loved by his friends but an object of aversion for his wife. How did that happen? The cause of it his male companions fail to understand—

You knew him, and you must have known his eyes—
How deep they were, and what a velvet light
Came out of them when anger or surprise,
Or laughter, or Francesca, made them bright.

Through the unexplained working of her feminine
over-sensibility or morbid pre-disposition, Francesca
came to fearing his strange eyes, especially after a portrait of him had been made where she thought she could
detect an uncanny look.

The painter put the devil in those eyes,
Unless the devil did, and there he stayed;
And then the lady fled from paradise;
And there's your fact. The lady was afraid.

Thus we are made to wonder at woman's unfathomable
headiness, which may bring ruin to a man, without leaving him a chance to grasp a plank of safety.

The portrait of Tasker Norcross—not a mere sketch,
like the preceding ones, but a full-length likeness—
creates a vivid interest for a character which is a blank,
a nonentity, an empty name.[1] The personality of the
narrator, Ferguson, fascinates us by its frankness and
outspoken sincerity. The poet lends him a vitality
which stands in striking contrast to the limp flabbiness
of the original of the portrait. His eyes, especially,
seem to express his soul, yet with a tinge of strange
contradiction:

[1] The idea, taken from Hawthorne's *Christmas Banquet,* grows
from a mere hint, provided by the novelist, into an elaborate portrait,
full of psychological complexity and living humanity.

126

> I could feel his eyes,
> And they were like two cold inquiring points
> Of a sharp metal. When I looked again,
> To see them shine, the cold that I had felt
> Was gone to make way for a smouldering
> Of lonely fire that I, as I knew then,
> Could never quench with kindness or with lies.

Not only has Ferguson the power to dissect souls as with a surgeon's knife, but his passion for breathing the full breath of life breeds in him indignant contempt for the glaring show of an existence without any moral or intellectual energy. He is an apostle of the American gospel of spiritual strenuousness, without which life is not worth living and man disowns his divine origin. We may see in him a belated son of the Puritans, who cannot any longer stick to any definite creed, but proclaims the need of an aim higher than vegetative growth or luxurious fattening. To live without a principle is to revile oneself to the level of the brute: let it be religious, moral or artistic, but something touched with the spark of the human divine. Let man find in soul-betterment the meaning of himself and of his relations to the world:

> Honor that is a friend begets a friend.
> Whether or not we love him, still we have him;
> And we must live somehow by what we have,
> Or then we die. If you say chemistry,
> Then you must have your molecules in motion,
> And in their right abundance. Failing either,
> You have not long to dance. Failing a friend,
> A genius, or a madness, or a faith

> Larger than desperation, you are here
> For as much longer than you like as may be.

This is Robinson at his best: philosophical poetry with the true ring of spiritual aspiration; a thoroughly modern largeness of thought; moral endeavor without moralizing; and withal the naturalness and ease of familiar dialogue; the Robinsonian excellence of verbal felicity, simplicity in dignity, and a superb marshalling of the elementary ingredients of speech into subtle delicacy and loftiness of phrase.

Ferguson is hard in his denunciation of those who wear the outward appearance of manhood, lacking the while what should animate the machine and give it its distinctive humanity. But his harshness is justified by the irritating conceit of the spiritually deficient:

> You have known
> All round you, all your days, men who are nothing—
> Nothing, I mean, so far as time tells yet
> Of any other need it has of them
> Than to make sextons hardy—but no less
> Are to themselves incalculably something,
> And therefore to be cherished. God, you see,
> Being sorry for them in their fashioning,
> Indemnified them with a quaint esteem
> Of self, and with illusions long as life. . . .

The thoughtful mood of the passage, which applies to universal man, irrespective of time and place, suggests the epithet "classic," to characterize it, although there is in the form all the novelty, boldness and pith that a

128

Byron, for instance, put in the biting sarcasm of Don Juan. The broad humanity of the content detracts nothing from the concreteness of the expression. The poet does not even refrain from what the classics called "the low," sure as he is to raise the commonplace to literary dignity by the grace of the word arrangement. To wit, this remark of the poet, qualifying Ferguson's harshness:

> Skin most of us of our mediocrity,
> We should have nothing then that we could scratch.

For such men as Norcross, the arts have no meaning. He can only wonder in amazement at

> strangers who forget
> Their sorrows and their failures and themselves
> Before a few mysterious odds and ends
> Of marble carted from the Parthenon.

How could the work of poets have any meaning for a man whose

> tethered range
> Was only a small desert. Kings of song
> Are not for thrones in deserts. Towers of sound
> And flowers of sense are but a waste of heaven
> Where there is none to know them from the rocks
> And sand-grass of his own monotony,
> That makes earth less than earth.

This last quotation affords a fair example of the way Robinson enlivens thought with imagery. The image is broad and complex, but is developed with consistency, a sure grasp of the concrete details and a supreme skill in bringing together the literal and the figurative meaning—that is in transferring thought from the spiritual to the material plane, or, in other cases, things from the concrete to the abstract—which is the highest office of poetry. The image is sometimes compressed in two lines:

> He could see stars,
> On a clear night, but he had not an eye
> To see beyond them. . . .

or

> He could eat food of which he knew the savor,
> But had no palate for the Bread of Life.

In the best passages, the image or the idea is couched in so apt words, and there is such an easy and sure correspondence between sense and sound, that the lines are a delight for the mind. By the freshness and perfect fitness of his vocabulary, as well as the inner logic and smooth harmony of his thought, Robinson demonstrates that there is such a thing as music of the intellect.

This is not the whole story of Tasker Norcross. I shall give later the key to this strange character, so startling in its nullity.

Robinson occasionally borrowed characters from history or legend. He did not shirk difficulties, for he went straight to some of the greatest figures recorded in the world-annals. We reserve his portrayal of Napoleon and of Rembrandt for our study of his humorous poetry, for he picked up circumstances of the lives of these great men that place them in a peculiar light, ruffled with ripples of grim pleasantry, that cover deep philosophical insight. Lazarus, Shakespeare and John Brown, on the other hand, are presented in their wonted appearance, in situations that set off their traditional human significance.

Lazarus, after his coming to life again, stands alone, wrapped in a long mantle with the hood on, at the twilight hour, shunned by all because of the fear he inspires. Even Mary and Martha hesitate to approach him, not repelled so much by the horror of death, which keeps away the vulgar, as shrinking from what he may have to tell of the life beyond the grave. This mysterious suspense resolves itself into tragic emotion when Lazarus finally overcomes his shyness and speaks. He has nothing to say of the beyond, but he sadly grieves for being back in this world, after having come so near the threshold of heaven. He saw the Lord weep when He raised him from the dead. Were those tears shed in despair or in hope? The whole poem is suffused with pathos of pure spiritual quality.

Only a master of delineation could approach a towering figure of the intellectual world like Shakespeare and succeed in enlarging the vision we have of him. He did not attempt to survey Shakespeare's colossal outlay or to appraise the merits of his plays. His purpose is to make us see the man, with his greatness and his hu-

131

manity, as he lived in the eyes of his contemporaries. The portrait is drawn by a dramatic story-teller, whose scholarship remains in the background, yet ever ready to provide some learned detail and to breathe in enthusiasm for the pre-eminency of literary genius. The title is *Ben Jonson Entertains a Man from Stratford*. It is an animated monologue of Ben Jonson telling his guest, an alderman of Stratford-on-Avon, over their cups, what he knows and thinks of the great dramatist. The scene is informal, the tone familiar, the mood of the speaker slightly humorous, as befits the occasion and the temper of the keen-witted playwright. The figure of Shakespeare gradually emerges from his speech in a living glow of genial splendor. Ben Jonson, who wrote comedies and tragedies by rule and precept, cannot refrain from some mild censure:

> . . . I tell him he needs Greek;
> I'll talk of rules and Aristotle with him. . . .

But his general attitude is one of devout and unreserved admiration. Sometimes he expresses his reverence, as a comrade of the stage may do, with droll familiarity. Thus when he playfully comments on what connects Shakespeare with common humanity:

> He must have had a father and a mother—
> In fact I've heard him say so—and a dog,
> As a boy should, I venture; and the dog,
> Most likely, was the only man who knew him.

132

Or when he speaks of his relations to women in his younger days,

> They've had him dancing till his toes were tender,
> And he can feel 'em now, come chilly rains.

Or again when he describes his effervescent brain, seething with the fever of creation:

>   . . . though to see him,
> You'd never guess what's going on inside him.
> He'll break out some day like a keg of ale
> With too much independent frenzy in it.

Generally his worshipful respect of the great man expresses itself with noble gravity. What if Shakespeare knows no rules but his own?

> He treads along through Time's old wilderness
> As if the tramp of all the centuries
> Had left no roads—and there are none, for him.

His friends are awed by his sombre moods for:

>   he has dreams
> Were fair to think on once, and all found hollow.
> He knows how much of what men paint themselves
> Would blister in the light of what they are. . . .

But how wonderful his return to intellectual buoyancy:

> To-day the clouds are with him, but anon
> He'll out of 'em enough to shake the tree
> Of life itself and bring down fruit unheard-of—
> And, throwing in the bruised and whole together,

133

Prepare a wine to make us drunk with wonder:
And if he live, there'll be a sunset spell
Thrown over him as over a glassed lake
That yesterday was all a black wild water.

Thus the gigantic genius of Shakespeare overpowers
Ben's mind and becomes doubly impressive through the
glow of his imaginative wonder and the warmth of his
admiring friendship. We seem to feel the direct impact of Shakespeare's glory, not as it came down to us
incased in the Pantheon of ages, but as if we had lately
seen the first performance of the great plays. We feel
as if we had elbowed Shakespeare in the street yesterday, when we read:

> . . . there shines out of him again
> An aged light that has no age or station—
> The mystery that's his—a mischievous
> Half-mad serenity that laughs at fame
> For being won so easy. . . .

Such power to endue with life the King of dramatic
genius, in the truth of his intellectual might, sweeping
prestige, and radiating personality, stamps Robinson a
great poet. There is no less suppleness than force in
his genius, for he can leap over the centuries and take
from American history, at the momentous period of the
conflict between North and South, a character that
stood, in the eyes of the North, as the incarnation of
vindictive justice and fanatic righteousness. In a letter
supposed to be written by John Brown to his wife, on
the eve of his execution, the poet adds the strength of his

pathetic doubt to the religious fervor and spirit of sacrifice that animated the frantic martyr for the cause of humanity.

Character-drawing, when it bears the physical and moral fullness, the wealth of psychological truth and the tragic force, which Robinson puts in his portraits, needs only to be incorporated to an action to expand into dramatic narrative. The latter *genre,* as the poet conceives it, is nothing but character-drawing moved from the static to the dynamic stage. He draws up a story— generally the bare outline of a plot—simple enough not to absorb the reader's attention, yet sufficient to bring in a succession of situations and attitudes. Psychological analysis remains his chief object. His main preoccupation is with the gathering impetus of a master-passion, its progress through subtle phases of development until it reaches its climax in thought or action, its growth from mood to mood leading up to a happy or a tragic ending where the spiritual elements are fully revealed in repose or in heart-rending intensity. As Robinson understands human nature, this means an acute searching of the obscure ways of the subconscious gradually dawning into clear consciousness. The narrative is less a tale of events—although some sequence of episodes is necessary to provide a guiding thread— than an adumbration of the mysteries of the cognizant and sentient being that is man.

Annandale, an idealist, a poet and self-analyst, has just lost his young wife. He is introduced to us on the

135

day of her burial, when he has come back to his empty home and sees all the familiar objects draped in sadness. The situation is pathetic. We are made to feel it by the haunting lyrical burden that recurs wistfully:

> And they had buried her that afternoon,
> Under the tight-screwed lid of a long box,
> Under the earth, under the leaves and snow.

Mournful regret is the feeling that crystallises in his consciousness. It creates the atmosphere in which will soon grow the complex activities of his mind. For grief is only one element—apparently the outstanding element—of his mental disturbance. He is assailed besides by subconscious intuitions that cross his brain in fitful starts. Now one wave of feeling, now another, rises for a moment to the surface: he is rocked to and fro as they emerge, and but dimly grasps their meaning. We are gradually taken into his confidence and darkly peer into the contradictions of his soul, just as he himself becomes darkly conscious of the struggle between his vocal reason and the mute aspirations of his inarticulate self. The ups and downs of his mood are rendered with a keen sensitiveness to the fluctuations of feeling which toss man on the ground-swell of deep emotion. Not only does the poet penetrate into some of the most subtle truths of the human heart, but he does it by sly approaches and tentative probings, as if commanded by the very rhythm of the heart's agitation. It is a rare example of how much psychological analysis and the discovery of the subconscious have enriched

136

modern literature. Robinson handles the mental microscope with superior skill and infallible surety, while remaining a master poet, full of delicate sympathy, moved by exquisite feelings and possessed of the most winning magic of phrase.

Annandale feels the desolate emptiness of the world around him, bereaved of the being that gave it significance. Yet

> there was
> A doubt, a pitiless doubt, a plunging doubt,
> That struck him, and upstartled, when it struck,
> The vision, the old thought in him.

He had written a book, unpublished, unknown to his wife, hardly known to himself, a book in which the poet dormant in him had couched in words that he had never read again, indited under the impulse of an exterior force, his ideal of love and beauty. His young wife might have been one of the inspirers of this lyrical outpouring, but not the sole inspirer, for the poem transcended the reach of any one passion and the seductiveness of any one woman. And now the weird appeal of what he had put in that book comes back to him as in a dream.

The poet mysteriously hints, in his tentative way (so effective to disclose the dim realities of the subconscious) at the indistinct call of Life, which makes itself heard to the young widower, even at the moment when he believes himself crushed by the cruel blow. This is not what conventional poems or novels have accustomed

us to.   But this is one side of the truth, of a truth that
goes beyond the superficialities of rose-colored literature, down to the hard and cold bedrock laved by the
subcurrents of the soul.   It may seem to sweep away the
halo of idealism which generations of gentle dreamers
have woven around our emotions.   But it is no perverse
desecration of holy things; for sentimental idealism did
nothing but cover over, with an imaginative, illusory
cloak, the Life-Force, which, even when unrecognized,
irresistibly asserts its rights.   It is the tread of this
Force that Annandale feels obscurely invading his desolate heart.

> He knew the loss—therefore it puzzled him
> That he should sit so long there as he did,
> And bring the whole thing back—the love, the trust,
> The pallor, the poor face, and the faint way
> She last had looked at him—and yet not weep.

The romantic attitude of life-long attachment to the
dead beloved had its beauty, and is, to some degree,
rooted in the depths of the human heart.   But literary
fiction has given it an exalted character which modern
realism is not prone to cherish.   Robinson, as we shall
see, makes a sharp difference between a man's and a
woman's grief in bereavement: the psychological and
dramatic interest of the poem partly rests on this contrast.   In the case of the man, psychological analysis
and realism rightly attribute more strength to the vital
instincts, subterraneously groping their way to light,
than to mourning grief.   In this Robinson is mod-

ern, and he is American; for it is in America, if anywhere, that the Life-Force—energy, will-to-live, desire for action—makes itself heard. There is no lack of pathos in the situation, for the struggle between the haunting regret for the lost love and the growing desire for recovery is one of the most moving trials the human heart may go through. There is no lack of idealism; for the bereaved man puts the whole strength of his reason and of his conscious will in the contest against the leagued powers of nature and of his imagination, working in his subliminal self. In fact, what we have here is a dramatic opposition of the older with the newer idealism, the former being more faithful to solemn loyalties, the latter more sensitive to the beauty of nature's ways. Grief and despair are negative: they suited a state of mind that tended to ascetic denial and resigned contemplation. Hope and will-to-live are positive: they are more likely to be the gospel of an age of large ambitions and vast achievements. But the modernism and Americanism of the latter conception do not preclude poetry. The inner conflict that takes place in the soul of Annandale is fraught with emotional and intellectual beauty.

The character feels dawning in him an imperative, uncalled for desire, a spontaneous, instant urge, that sends him through alternate qualms of despondency and hope:

> . . . he was lost.
> And yet he was not lost: he was astray—
> Out of his life and in another life;

And in the stillness of this other life
He wondered and he drowsed. He wondered when
It was, and wondered if it ever was
On earth that he had known the other face—
The searching face, the eloquent, strange face—
That with a sightless beauty looked at him
And with a speechless promise uttered words
That were not the world's words, or any kind
That he had known before. . . .

It was not the face of any individual woman—not yet, at least. But the face was there, mutely luring him to question his sorrow, while his sorrow bade him to question his hope. The pathos of the situation is rendered more poignant by the simple directness of the style. The expression is so unaffected, so free from apparent artifice, that it seems to be the very language of the tormented heart, disburdening itself of its anguish, in all sincerity.

The second part of the poem tells the story of Damaris, the widow of Argan, when, several years after her cruel loss, she comes to meet Annandale. Her grief is still fresh and stinging; it is a woman's grief, a grief that is the law of her heart, as love had been the life of her being. When Argan was on his death-bed, she had sworn an oath never to wed another man. Now she is bound by her truthful feelings as well as by truthfulness to her word. Yet she has seen Annandale and she has read his book. She seemed to detect in his looks a sign of interest for her, and, in her naïve woman's conceit, she believed that the book was written for her and that *the face* is her face. In spite of her own will, a new feeling makes its way into her heart. It is not, as in the case of Annandale, an ideal yearning that urges her; but an attachment for the living man, whom she admires and all but loves without confessing it to herself.

Under circumstances, then, very different from those we have met before, and yet similar, Damaris will go through the very ordeal which Annandale has known, in the grip of the Life-Force. Her tragedy wears a pathos of its own, based on the traits of her womanly nature. Sentiment is stronger in her than the imagination. It is not a dim hankering after the past and a vague yearning for an imprecise future, that agitate her: she feels at once clinched to the old love by her fidelity and her promise, and urged on by the impulse of the new love.

> She knew that love
> Was true, that he was true, that she was true;
> And should a death-bed snare that she had made
> So long ago be stretched inexorably
> Through all her life, only to be unspun
> With her last breathing?

She reasons with herself; she remembers that her dying husband, in his agony, moved his lips, as if to speak, when she took the oath. Was it not to refuse the solemn pledge? She has a notion (or rather the poet has it for her, but how true to psychological truth!) that she is not the same woman now as she was when tears filled her eyes, by Argan's death-bed. Robinson is too keen an observer not to make use here of one of the most

141

striking discoveries of psychology, namely, that there is no such thing as one unmovable ego, but that we pass successively through various personalities, as we go through various phases of experience.

> And who was *she?*   The woman she had known—
> The woman she had petted and called "I"—
> The woman she had pitied, and at last
> Commiserated for the most abject
> And persecuted of all womankind,—
> Could it be she that had sought out the way
> To measure and thereby to quench in her
> The woman's fear—the fear of her not fearing?

Finally, what was to happen takes place.   Annandale's looks of love, the flaming eloquent pages of the book, that she more and more believes to be addressed to her, overcome her last hesitations:

> For now there were no wretched quivering strings
> That held her to the churchyard any more:
> There were no thoughts that flapped themselves like bats
> Around her any more. . . .   And the truth,
> Like silence after some far victory,
> Had come to her, and she had found it out
> As if it were a vision, a thing born
> So suddenly!—just as a flower is born,
> Or as a world is born—so suddenly.

There is a marked originality and novelty in the manner of the narrative, as well as in the analysis of the feelings and in the treatment of the situations.   Under it all, there runs a deep current of broad and universal humanity, which we also find in a story of haunting fear, with a tinge of madness in it: *Avon's Harvest.*

The poet wants to interest us in his friend Avon, whose eyes burn with an unnatural fire, due probably to some grave distemper in his constitution or in his mind. We are first made to see the outward aspect of the man, once a cheerful companion and a gentle husband, now a living wreck wrapped in a sombre glow, diffused from his incandescent eyes. He buries himself in silence. He

> Fed with his unrevealing reticence
> The fire of death we saw that horribly
> Consumed him while he crumbled and said nothing.

What is the mental mystery that lurks behind the smouldering embers in his looks? The man has not a very large share of intelligence, as his wife jocularly remarked when she had still enough freedom of mind to laugh. But now the fear that has settled in his face communicates itself to her, and the poet wonders what unknown danger hangs over those two unfortunate creatures. One day, Avon manifests a desire to pour his secret in his friend's bosom, tête-à-tête, with the door locked on all intruders, not even his wife being admitted. The mystery is going to be solved. But not at once. The facts—that is the strange growth of the man's distraction—will be disclosed in a skilful gradation that takes us, as Avon's confidence proceeds, from wonder to anxiety, and from pity to horror. The poet's artistry somewhat recalls the manner of Edgar A. Poe, by the

143

careful successive approaches toward the crowning revelation and by the concentration of interest on the topic that more and more engrosses our mind. Descriptions of the outward bewildered state of the man alternate with vivid pictures of the inner tragedy, and the effect of his narrative on the listening friend is recorded with peerless mastery. Robinson has a surer grasp than Poe of the secret workings of the soul. His tale consists of purely psychical elements. When, at the end, a ghost is introduced, we feel that it is not a cheap romantic device, but an exteriorisation of the inward vision, a filmy projection into the twilight mist of the feverish hallucination that floats in the sick man's subconsciousness. Robinson remembers the blood-curdling sights of hellish horrors that used to appal the early Puritans, and he makes Avon an heir to their gloomy moping. His manner suggests a combination of Hawthorne's analysis with Poe's spectral creations, with more of the *Scarlet Letter* than of the *House of Usher*. Yet the resulting effect is entirely his own. Avon's madness arises from a disturbed conscience, whose self-torturing propensity is magnified by his diseased condition. The distemper grows from Avon's school-boy days, when he conceived a groundless hatred for one of his classmates, to his manhood, when his deranged feelings, under the stress of his aroused conscience, changed into remorse and then into haunting fear. The last scene is laid in a typically American setting (a camp on the shore of one of the Maine lakes) whose beauty enhances the ghostly catastrophe. In a horrible waking

nightmare, he saw the phantom of the wronged class-
mate stand up before him, in the pale gleam of a flickering candle

> Then he caught
> The shadowy glimpse of an uplifted arm,
> And a moon-flash of metal. That was all. . . .

In the night after the narration of this dismal vision,
Avon died. The doctor spoke of an aneurism, but he
died in fact of his fear. His conscience had killed him.

In the shorter poems, Robinson's power to compress
in a few pages or in a few stanzas the drama of agitated
or distorted souls can hardly be surpassed. The Unforgiven is a husband who committed no other crime
than letting his once romantic love for his wife subside
with time to a sober affection, more in keeping with her
faded looks:

> And she, the unforgiving, hates him
> More for her lack than for her loss.

The clergyman who had married Sainte-Nitouche and
lost her, sought in a redoubled intensity of religious
fervor a consolation for his bereavement. Did he find
truth, or half-truth, in his faith? Was it the old love
that revived in his sacerdotal devotion? He died in
peace and his example ought to lighten the way of those
who can, as he did, substitute ardent belief for ardent
love.

The Mill is a striking instance of how pathos can be
worked, not so much from the fabric of a tale, as from
the atmosphere of tragedy raised about a tale, accord-

GOSHEN COLLEGE LIBRARY

ing to the "inferential" method of Robinson. A miller, running a small mill in the New England country, has lost all hope, as we make out, of competing with the big industrial plants of the West. He had exclaimed, in his wife's hearing: "There are no millers any more!" and had gone out. Alarmed at not seeing him turn in for tea, his wife repaired to the mill.

> Sick with a fear that had no form
>   She knew that she was there at last;
> And in the mill there was a warm
>   And mealy fragrance of the past.
> What else there was would only seem
>   To say again what he had meant;
> And what was hanging from a beam
>   Would not have heeded where she went.

In this mysterious, thrilling way, we are made aware of the desperate act the miller had committed to put an end to the hopeless struggle against odds. In the same indirect manner, full of pathetic reticence, we are led to picture to ourselves the last scene of the drama. That thing—once her beloved husband—strikes the wife aghast.

> And if she thought it followed her,
>   She may have reasoned in the dark
> That one way of the few there were,
>   Would hide her and would leave no mark:
> Black water, smooth above the weir
>   Like starry velvet in the night,
> Though ruffled once, would soon appear
>   The same as ever to the sight.

It is not given to many poets thus to draw pathetic effects from a few allusions so aptly selected and expressed as to suggest the facts of a dramatic story, without any flat enumeration of details, and forcibly to bring out the emotions latent in the intimated facts. This can be done only by a powerful mind, both introspective and creative, that encompasses in a single act of thought the logic of the will, the reverberations of the feelings, the waves of obscure intuitions and sudden resolves, the virtualities of passion, enthusiasm, or despair, implied in a situation. What gives Robinson's dramatic narratives or sketches so much force is the intellectual excellence, that imparts also such vigor of outline and such depth of moral significance to his characters. As he builds a plot by setting up only its salient constituents, so he portrays a personage in misty tints, with a few simplified strokes, with a delicate sense of the finesse of physiognomy and of the mellowness of life. His narratives, scenes and likenesses are interpretations: they search the depths of man's psychical being, explain actions by motives and analyze feelings in their remotest ramifications. His psychology is that of a keen observer, of a reflective spectator of the human drama, of a sure appraiser of moral values. He may be sometimes carried by his bias for subtle analysis to refine beyond what the average reader can enjoy: but this occasional defect (which does not impair the wholeness of his poetical insight) is amply compensated by the exquisiteness of his delineations and the novelty of his outlook. As to the reproach, that was

147

made him, to evince a morbid preference for the gloomy side of life and the dispiriting, unbalanced manifestations of human behavior, it does not bear examination: for it is in the intense motions of the sensibility, in the dark broodings of the intellect, in the grim struggles of the conscience, that human nature, like the earth-crust under pressure of the central fire, breaks up in revealing rifts.

Whatever the subtlety or the sombreness of Robinson's intellectualism, it bears the mark of unmistakable human truth. Grave or grim earnestness is the necessary condition of tragic force. Robinson's inspiration (except when it throbs in lyrical fervor or relents in sarcastic humor) is essentially tragic. His dramatic vein, none the less, admits of peaceful moments of calm, where the winning qualities that we admire in his lyrics distil their penetrating charm. His endings not unfrequently subside to serene or solemn repose. His form, delicately simple, gracefully sinuous, gently winding in successive advances and recoils, like the leisurely gait of his thoughtful mind, chastened, reserved, closely adapted to the ideas and feelings, moves in an atmosphere of harmony. His perfect control of his ample intellectual resources, of his rich imaginative inventiveness, of his power of sympathy and of his means of expression shows itself in the easy flow of his rhymed stanzas as well as in his blank-verse periods, enhanced by the sober quality of self-restraint and bathed in a sensuous glow of color and of plastic beauty.

It suited his modesty to speak diffidently of the poet's labor,

In Art's long hazard, where no man may choose
Whether he play to win or toil to lose.

But it is ours to say that a kind Fate led his hand,
whether in play or toil, to lay down the stake of his
exquisite genius—and win.

Cavender's House (published in 1929) is a new departure in Robinson's treatment of narrative poetry.
By its materials—the characters, the plot, the setting
and the local coloring—it is germane to *Roman Bartholow* and might have been another metrical novel of
contemporary manners. But the poet chose to raise
it to an imaginative plane, where the real and the unreal combine to make a gossamer drama of stirring
novelty. The emotional tone is pitched so high that
it lends itself naturally, as it were, to a visionary trans-
ference. Facts borrowed from life and feelings true
to psychological truth are gradually floated, without
losing their consistence or aching vividness, into the
misty medium of a dreamlike aura. Like Coleridge,
Robinson succeeded, through intense contemplation of
the borderland between the material and immaterial, in
creating that "momentary suspension of disbelief,"
which carries us into the awful regions of the spiritual.
The fantastic here is nothing but the imaginative subli-
mation of actual soul-experiences under the shock of
a fearful inner impact. Artistically, it is a heightened
form of pathos, wrapped in wonder; esthetically, it is
a hallucination projected into a myth.

Cavender, a weak sensualist given to fits of violent
passion, after jilting his young wife, was led to believe
from her ironical contempt that she had revenged her-

self by flying into another man's arms. One night, on the garden-terrace at the back of their house, a stormy discussion ended in a savage onslaught of the man against the woman, in which she toppled over the railing and fell on the rocks forty feet below. There was a presumption of suicide and Cavender did nothing to dispel the city-folks' surmise. He started on a thirteen years' travel to distant countries. But his conscience harrowed him all the time. He came back to the deserted house and there, in the dim light of the moon, saw before him his wife, placid, unchanged, her sarcastic smile softened with pity.

The poem begins on that night of the return home, in a ghostly setting of darkness and fear, with the memories of the past brought back to appalling vividness. A dialogue engages between the culprit and the phantom of his victim. There remains in him enough of his puritan education to make remorse cruelly active, but his will is too feeble to face the logical consequences of the deed. There is one thing he wants to know, one question he insists on asking, one chance of evasion he tries to grasp. Did Laramie actually retaliate, paying back treason for treason? Can he find a retrospective justification for the murder? In his distraction, he presses the dire question on the unreal Laramie, as if she were not a mere projection of his own thoughts. The situation, with its fantastic coloring and ghastly breathlessness, is intensely dramatic. We are left to believe, until an advanced stage of the action, that Laramie is a living survival of herself, miraculously saved and called there by some thought-message. She will not—indeed, cannot—answer the question. Hers is to play the part of justice—not implacable, for her Christian faith reserves a way to salvation, if the guilty one muster courage to bow to God's decree. After pathetically struggling to repulse her intimations—which are but the voice of moral inevitability making itself audible in his inmost being—he yields, unwilling to let go the last hope left to him in the beyond. We understand that he will surrender himself up to expiation.

The conception of the subject is eminently poetical. Through the power of the imagination, the torture of a sinful soul, tracked by remorse and restlessly fretting to escape, is concretized into a dramatic action, where personified moral forces assume the appearance of the murderer and the murdered one, returned to life to utter hard but necessary words of awful truth. The vision is introduced with masterly skill by an insensible shifting from factual data to the soul-contest embodied in the ghostly dialogue. The unreal character of the woman is drawn with so much plausibility, that it seems to be present bodily, all its borrowed vitality centering in the imperious glare of its eyes. Robinson achieved the difficult feat of making a ghost live, by sheer strength of psychological insight and dramatic creation. The shivering gloom, the thrill of vague apprehension, the carefully elaborated details—such as Laramie's sudden looming out of nothingness, the muffled resonance of her voice, the strange lustre of her white hands crossed on her lap—place the scene, from the outset, in an atmos-

phere of hallucination. We hesitate between belief
and unbelief, we are moved and bewildered—until the
spell works irresistibly and we yield to the mystery.

What gives to the feelings and thoughts their force
of contagion is the fact that they contain the sum total
of a long experience of pain brought to a climax in a
flash of divinatory consciousness. Laramie's presence
is due to the splitting up of Cavender's personality; her
speech proceeds from one moiety of his divided conscience, at the hour when stale self-questioning and
incipient self-abhorrence, not yet quite acknowledged
by reason, give him a retrospective comprehension of
his wife's ordeal and make him realize what her attitude
would be, if she were there before him, uttering words
that are not of this world. His fevered brain projects
outside the image of the dead one, superhumanly composed, and she becomes the symbol of justice pressing
its claim and demanding punishment. There is no violent outburst, no loud indictment, no melodrama. The
inner consciousness of the helpless wretch is gradually
disclosed, with its anomalies and contradictions, never
trespassing out of psychological or moral truth, never
transgressing the laws of moderate expression. The
whole drama, with its intense human agony seems re-
moved to a dim distance, whence the voices are wafted
on the wind through whirls of mist. A ray of Christian
mercy and hope softens the distressing situation, al-
lowing for a catharsis which leaves us in an appeased
mood to gather in our emotions and reflections.

There is pathos in that division of Cavender's soul

and the transfer of his better self to his wife, brought back from the dead to hold up the mirror where truth is reflected. There is mystery in the temporary confusion of existence and non-existence. There is wonder in the dramatic effectiveness of the dialogue, which modifies reality the better to extract from it its full substance. The blending of the natural and the supernatural enhances with awful solemnity the haunting thought of guilt and the insistent appeal of the conscience. Genius reveals itself in that intuitive vision which incorporates moral values in living symbols. It brings into prominence, by means properly pertaining to art, the obscure causes of crime and the mysterious nature of the conscience. The characters hover between this world and the world beyond in a shimmering light, shot through by weirdly luminous streaks. The style abounds in touches of decorous, sober beauty, which match the broad simplicity and powerful restraint of the theme of the poem, and are like the features of a face where the motions of the soul inscribe themselves with appealing expressiveness.

Robinson shows a capacity of sympathy which is neither narrow nor vulgar. It is wide enough to include a murderer in the human family. Cavender is not presented like a senseless, infuriated brute; he is a weak-willed man too easily carried out of himself by passion, but accessible to moral suffering and capable of repentance, when time and reason have relaxed his hard self-delusion. The same respect for psychological truth guards Robinson from vulgarity. He does not harp upon the string of abused or persecuted innocence. Sinless, perhaps, is Laramie in her soul and in her flesh (she cannot tell him, being only a projection of his own tortured thoughts) but she is not presented as a claimant to heroic virtue. She had not been above the human, too human, desire of getting even with her husband, in her quiet way, by her equivocal attitude and sarcastic smile. Her playing with the fire had started the conflagration. Thus we see Robinson steering clear of the romantic artificiality which extols the good and reviles the bad, without shadings, for the sake of violent contrasts. He is a realist as well as a visionary. His strength lies in the truthfulness of his observation, not in sensational exaggerations.

He likewise eschews the literature of edification. What remains in him of his puritan origin makes him regard moral issues, but he does not emphasize them inartistically. He looks facts in the face, eager to seize their full ethical significance, without assuming the preacher's tone. At heart a classic, he appropriates from romantic esthetics what can be conciliated with broad reasonableness and an eclectic taste for beauty. Hence that refraction of reality through the prism of the imagination, that interpenetration of the visible and the invisible, that radiation of the life of the soul through an atmosphere of mystery. His poetry, deeply human in its inspiration, is leavened by a fecund breath of spirituality.

CHAPTER V

HUMOR

SMALL men are of one mood; big men welcome all the moods wherein human impulses and aspirations find themselves reflected. At his hours of solitary musing, Robinson hears the doleful whisper of love, or the deep-toned voice of death, or the mysterious call of destiny, and lyrical wistful stanzas sing in his mind. At his hours of sympathetic mental intercourse with the spirit of men and women, he calls up remembrances of characters he has known and human facts he has experienced, and indites interpretative and dramatic poetry. But the lyrical, the narrative or the dramatic forms are not the only channels of his creative imagination. There are hours when his sprightly intellect is aware of incongruities in individual minds that baffle reason, or of discrepancies in the social order that mar man's attempts at carrying out a seemly scheme of life. If he were the gloomy Puritan that some morose critics deem him to be, these flaws in the order of things would cause him to groan at the sorry mess men make of their opportunities. Instead, he smiles and points to the oddity of those unexpected halts and turns in the course of the world. He is a humorist.

His humor, it is true, is never a pure hilarious mood.

155

He is too much of a thinker not to see the deep signifi-cance of the bizarre in individuals or in society, and too much of an artist not to invest his jestful remarks with beauty. Robinson the humorist remains a keen analyst of psychological facts, a quick and sympathetic spec-tator of the pageant of life, a sure appraiser of philosoph-ical and ethical values and a coiner of harmonious and striking phrases. Without interfering in a didactic way, simply by the drift of the tale, the saliency of a few well-chosen features, the drollness of the coloring, the unexpectedness of the similes and images, the signi-ficance of the words, he brings out the inner meaning of a character or of an episode. The contradictions and contrasts that arouse his sense of humor are not mere signs of the whimsicality of persons or the instability of things. They afford him glimpses of a subcurrent of thought, of feeling or of human relationship that re-mains hidden to most of us beneath the surface-flow of perceptions, by the fact that our consciousness is a thrall to habit and routine, or too narrow to contain all the truth, or too hasty to take a comprehensive view of the entire reality.

Robinson's playful mood—as is the case with large minds—is one in which he achieves some of his most searching observations of moral and social man and reveals the most original aspects of his philosophy. His puritan education—powerless to smother his artistic temperament—stands him in good stead by inclining his mind to serious reflection, even when it feels prone to trifle with the odds and ends of human experience. He is guided by a strong sense of the spiritual unity of man, even when dealing with such exceptional beings as cranks, derelicts or riders of hobbies. He is prepared to discover sometimes in those stragglers on the margin of society a spark of spiritual flame, capable of illuminating by fits some obscure workings of the human mind or some dark relation of man's life to the life of the cosmos.

At other times, he sees, exemplified in exceptional individuals by the effect of distorted or arrested growth, mental deficiencies (to be found in reduced proportions in other men) which he exposes as legitimate objects of ridicule. His mirth then is so tempered with pity or so permeated with sympathy, that his gibes at such departures from balanced sanity or from the normal course of reason easily swerve to pathos and not seldom culminate in tragedy.

His humor can be sad or bitter; but he is not a wilful pessimist. The puritanical bent of his mind, modified by modern thought and by the urge of his poetical genius, leads him, in his handling of character or behavior, to take position against some of the typical puritan prejudices or shortcomings. Like Emerson (to whom he is much indebted), he is a son of the Puritans who has become anti-puritan. His thought, in his humorous as well as in his philosophical poems, is markedly spiritualistic, but without affiliation to any narrow orthodoxy. He is as averse to bigotry as to materialism. He derides the petty ridicules of blind worshippers as freely as he taunts the gross callousness of scoffers. There is a largeness in his outlook on life, when he indulges in cheerful abandon, that takes in all that is beautiful in nature and all that is gentle in man. He welcomes none of the exclusions of the Puritans, none of their shrinkings from their weak-willed brothers, none of their narrow ethical standards. The artist in him leads the philosopher by the hand and opens to him vistas of beauty and of sympathy in the sunlit places of the universe, or detects gleams of luminous shade where starvelings darkly grope their way.

He has not much in common with a puritan humorist like Carlyle. Carlyle forged his glittering steely style by dint of great hammer blows, but with little sense of beauty. His fiery soul yearned for ethical reform and for aristocratic repression of democracy with a passion which precluded individual sympathy. He was a humorist by his masculine handling of the picturesque and the grotesque, but quickly flew to violent outbursts that found expression in sarcasm, satire or bitter irony. Such is not the case with Robinson.

Robinson has many points of contact with Browning, who like himself is essentially an artist and whose humor has the breadth, variety and richness that go along with tolerance, open sympathy and many-sided interests. Robinson owes him much in the humorous, as well as in the other, sections of his work, having felt attracted by the dramatic narratives and psychological lyrics, for which English literature is particularly indebted to the creative genius of Browning. But Robinson follows Browning—as Tennyson followed Keats, or Browning himself did Shelley—without alienating his personality or his power of invention. While Browning borrowed characters and subjects from history, Robinson draws them from his own experience and from his knowledge of his neighbors. Although working in the same *genre,* the natures of the two poets are so wide apart that the products of their inspiration offer distinctly individual features. There is, in Browning, an overflowing, buoyant jollity that leads him often to assume a loud, boisterous tone, ringing with jocund strains, brimful of the sap of mirth. In another mood, he is carried to the other extreme and loads his humor with caustic quips and lashing gibes. At times, he fuses both manners and revels in capering, travestied farce. Robinson is much less inclined to clamorous exuberance or to sour tooth-gnashing. His humor may broaden to a laugh or concentrate in a thrust; but generally it bears the mild tone of subdued merriment or gentle criticism, streaked with delicate feelings or fine intellectual remarks. By the side of Browning's prancing phrases, bounding jokes or biting sarcasms, his form shows a reserve, a finish, which give it a highly artistic flavor and almost classic balance and self-restraint. He is anxious to avoid anything coarse in the expression or too harsh in the conception.

He is full of indulgence for those whose failings do no harm but to themselves and who diverge from the common path, not out of any wickedness, but because their originality cannot conform to the hard and fast canons of usage. Is not their very non-conformity an interesting proof of the power of self-determination that gives its significance to human individuality? Is it not possible for a keen-witted student of the ways of men to detect in the freaks or oddities of such outsiders fine points that enhance man's capacity to understand this world, or open new approaches to happiness? If their idiosyncrasies are only queer, let us enjoy their queerness. If there is a soft spot in their brains, which makes of them in some of their actions ludicrous puppets, let us smile at the emphasis that their words and gestures put on weaknesses all men are liable to. If their self-delusion, conceit or unguarded behavior exposes some silly trick of human folly, let us indulge through them in mild mockery of ourselves. From all those originals we may learn something about men, whether the perception of their ridicules sharpens our judgment, or the appreciation of their singularities enlarges our vision. It requires penetration to do either: Robinson facilitates the effort for us. He is an excellent manager of the side-shows of the world's fair. He selects good actors and gets up well-devised entertainments, made of mingled gaiety and pathos, with a delicate blending of keen characterisation and playful fantasy, all wrapped in thoughtful humor, now touched by mellow wisdom, now colored with stark realism, now illumined by flashes of lyrical beauty.

His humor may be a clear ripple of laughter. He pleasantly boasts of this propensity of his mind in a delightful little poem that may be placed as an epigraph at the beginning of this study. It is entitled *Momus,* and consists of three short stanzas, full of genuine mirth.

The tripping rhythm, the echo-like rhymes, the dog-
gerel flavor, the pretended impudence, all contribute to
enhance the quality of the stingless fun:

> "Who reads Byron any more?"—
> Shut the door,
> Momus, for I feel a draught;
> Shut it quick, for some one laughed.—
> "What's become of
> Browning? Some of
> Wordsworth lumbers like a raft?
>
> "What are poets to find here?"—
> Have no fear:
> When the stars are shining blue
> There will yet be left a few
> Themes availing—
> And these failing,
> Momus, there'll be you.

In this spirit of sportive merriment, Robinson composed some delightful portraits of funny masqueraders
on Life's stage. A white-haired widower, nicknamed
Old King Cole, cursed with two scape-grace sons, finds
consolation and forgetfulness in his pipe and bowl.
Some officious friends plague him with reports of the
scamps' evil doings; but he

> with many a puff
> That haloed his urbanity,
> Would smoke till he had smoked enough,

and enter into a lengthy explanation of his reasons to
remain cheerful, that would send his friends to sleep.

In contrast, Bokardo, a sour, cavilling failure, with something apparently pretty bad in his record, is almost too much even for his friends. One of them addresses him in would-be anger:

> Friends, I gather, are small things
> In an age when coins are kings;
> Even at that, one hardly flings
>   Friends before swine. . . .
> No offense to swine, as such . . .

But let the old maniac be careful, for the laws of life need to be dealt with cautiously,

> Xerxes, when he flogged the sea,
>   May've scared a fish.
> It's a comfort, if you like,
> To keep honor warm;
> But as often as you strike
>   The laws, you do no harm.
> To the laws, I mean. To you—
> That's another point of view.

Calling to memory a character and incidents that belong to his boyhood days, the poet portrays Uncle Ananias, an old teller of fibs, whom he places, with his gallery of fascinated hearers, in a lovely landscape, bright with the varied splendors of the seasons.

> His words were magic and his heart was true. . . .
> Of all authoritative liars, too,
>   I crown him loveliest. . . .
> With what superb magnificence and ease

He sinned enough to make the day sublime! . . .
All summer long we loved him for the same
Perennial inspiration of his lies;
And when the russet wealth of autumn came,
There flew but fairer visions to our eyes—
Multiple, tropical, winged with a feathery flame
    Like birds of paradise.

Only a lyrical poet like Robinson could clothe humor
in such delicate hues. His fancy again plays with
reminiscence, as he recalls Miniver Cheevy, an abortive
poet and dull dreamer of dreams, who gives himself airs
by descanting on the vulgarity of our age compared to
the age of romantic ladies and caracoling knights.

    Miniver cursed the commonplace
        And eyed a khaki suit with loathing;
    He missed the mediaeval grace
        Of iron clothing. . . .
    Miniver Cheevy, born too late,
        Scratched his head and kept on thinking;
    Miniver coughed, and called it fate,
        And kept on drinking.

Humor takes on a melancholy tinge in *Mr. Flood's
Party*. Old Eben Flood, who lived alone on the mountain side, had gone to town to buy a jug of ale. On his
way back, in the bright glow of the harvest moon, he
stops on the road and invites himself to quaff a draught.

Then, as a mother lays her sleeping child
Down tenderly, fearing it may awake,
He set the jug down slowly at his feet
With trembling care, knowing that most things break. . . .

163

By repeated invitations to himself, the dear old man drained the jug to the last drop, and there, alone, started singing,

Until the whole harmonious landscape rang.

The last lines intensify the note of sympathy that colors the whole poem:

There was not much that was ahead of him,
And there was nothing in the town below—
Where strangers would have shut the many doors
That many friends had opened long ago.

In *Isaac and Archibald,* the recollective mood takes the poet back to a hot day in August, when, a little boy of twelve, he accompanied old Isaac on a visit to his friend Archibald, as broken and tottering as he, living on his farm, two or three miles away. A few vivid strokes of description call up the landscape:

> We walked together down the River Road
> With all the warmth and wonder of the land
> Around us, and the wayside flash of leaves . . .

On the way, Isaac naïvely unconscious of what has happened to himself of late years, tells the boy of the sad change he notices in Archibald. Referring solely to his friend, he says, with moving concern, how pitiful it is

> To know that you are losing what was yours,
> To know that you are being left behind.

At Archibald's place, the host and his two visitors go down to the cellar where eight barrels lie in a row, containing cider which the owner declares "an honor to the fruit." A moment later, as Archibald and the boy are sitting by themselves, the old man improves the opportunity to disburden his mind of his anxious thoughts about Isaac:

> You have seen—
> Young as you are, you must have seen the strange
> Uncomfortable habit of the man?
> He'll take my nerves and tie them in a knot
> Sometimes, and that's not Isaac. I know that. . . .
> That's what it is: Isaac is not quite right. . . .

How truly human! It is excellent comedy—a snapshot of the lives of two old men, linked by true friendship, yet not so heroically devoted as not to point out a flaw in the other fellow or not to satisfy themselves that each keeps a superiority over the other. This is the sly way self will assert itself. Genuine humor, suffused with sympathy, gives the poet a sure insight into the truth of character and life's inner reality.

Sympathy also is the outstanding quality in the portrait of the man described in *Old Trails*. This friend of former days has no name. He is of the kind for which Robinson feels a certain partiality: failures, according to the ordinary standards of judgment, who yet have something in them that makes them likeable and interesting. This friend is an artist, conscious of lacking the strength of will which alone can secure success. His best years have passed, not void of thought, but barren of achievement. He says: "My dreams have all come true to other men." He hastens to relate his misadventures, for fear his friend may guess them, and remarks profoundly: "Though you are silent, what you say is true." He is at odds even with the things of ordinary life. At the tavern, he complains: "They chill drinks here with ice from hell!" Yet he cherished cheerful confidence in his star:

> Whether he knew or not, he laughed and dined
> With more of an immune regardlessness
> Of pits before him and of sands behind
> Than many a child at forty would confess.

Flammonde is also an artist in his way, not practicing poetry or painting, but an expert in the art of living. He came from foreign parts to the puritan village of Tilbury Town and raised there surprise and no small scandal by his desultory ease, careless elegance and indulgent geniality. A perfect gentleman, refined to his finger-tips, he made it his business to know men, probe their deeper nature, appraise their real worth and smooth their mutual relations. Of money, which the other citizens (as true Americans) worshipped devoutly, he showed princely disregard,

> And what he needed for his fee
> To live, he borrowed graciously.

A parasite, then? A dissembler, who strutted about the streets to conceal his beggarly condition? No: a teacher of the true meaning of humanity, a living example of what gentle manners and sociality may do to soften puritan harshness. He never uttered a word of censure, but quietly did things, that, if rightly understood, would have melted the heart and broadened the judgment of his fellow-townsmen. Is the town ever to stand aloof from the man and ever towards him "nourish an ethical unrest"? Or are they, in the long run, to share in the poet's opinion, expressed in the startling praise:

> Rarely at once will nature give
> The power to be Flammonde and live.

Thus Robinson's humor, when it implies reproof (as here with regard to the puritan population of the village), blames by indirection, avoiding angry or indignant indictment, keeping its poise, intimating its intention in the reserved tone that is the charm of urbane poetry.

He can sometimes sharpen his pen and use it to prick ballooned heads swollen with self-conceit or arrant selfishness. He does not do it often. In one case only does his arraignment of moral ugliness take on a bitter tang; and, in this case, he seems to be goaded to some degree of severity by the offensive sin of hypocrisy. Humor remains the dominant note, but there is a twist in the smile, that might, we feel, on a slight provocation, turn to a grin. The poet, it is true, does not speak in his own name. He makes Captain Craig—a queer philosophical ranter—draw the portrait of a self-seeking, self-pushing, silly woman, corrupted by money and dazzled by insolent prosperity. She

Giggles and eats and reads and goes to church,
Makes pretty little penitential prayers,
And has an eighteen-carat crucifix
Wrapped up in chamois-skin. She gives enough,
You say; but what is giving like hers worth?
What is a gift without the soul to guide it?
"Poor dears, and they have cancers?—Oh!" she says;
And away she works at that new altar-cloth
For the Reverend Hieronymus Mackintosh. . . .

Even when a few bristles stick out under the velvet, Robinson's humor is never coarse. How different his refined and subtle pleasantry from what passes current under the appellation of "American humor!" America is vast enough to harbor many descriptions of humor, as well as a variety of physical or intellectual types and a rich collection of literary tastes. There is no relationship between the boisterous exuberance of Mark Twain or the droll fun of Artemus Ward, who turn the world upside down or pull men inside out to produce rollicking laughter, and the delicate touch of the poet who sifts experience and scrutinizes mental complexions to contrast the show of pretenses and the reality of achievements, or to bare the anatomy of the brain hidden under the made-up face. The former are professional mirthgivers, who amusingly distort facts by huge exaggeration or sheer absurdity; the latter is an analyst and a thinker who chooses to impart psychological or moral truth in an entertaining way by making us smile at the world and at ourselves. The humor of buoyancy affords a moment's loud enjoyment to those who seek relief from hard work and plodding routine: it is a cheap help to mental refreshment, in the manner a shower-bath relaxes the muscles of a football player. The humor of finesse brings rest by setting the brain in motion: it is a change of pursuits which unbends the tension of an active mind and gives it new vigor. Mere rowdy fun shakes us with waves of laughter, which soon flatten down like the surface of a lake when the storm is past. Intellectually significant humor imprints permanent and substantial marks on receptive minds like the gullies which soft rains carve on fruitful soil.

There are various ways for the thoughtful humorist to impress our consciousness. He can, as he feels inclined, take the carping or the insinuating tone, flaunt raillery or suggest ridicule, openly share in his own gaiety, or, in a sad mood, wrap sorrow-laden mirth in an atmosphere of pathos. One of the most penetrating forms of humor is dramatic humor. Through it, human pain expresses itself without strained accents. Wounded hearts or sacrificed souls claim our sympathy without indulging in elegiac lament. Suffering wears the outward appearance of equanimity. The restraint the characters impose upon themselves compels us to the same self-infliction: we are gripped by mute sadness, while ostensibly invited to laugh. Irony in such a case is the prevailing tone of the characters—often biting irony, which, under cover of a smile, sinks into the heart and burns it with slow fire. The stress may be too hard for human strength to bear: there madness lies. Tragic humor is not seldom tinged with the dark hues of distrac-

tion.   Shakespeare made a masterly use of it.   In a less
sombre key, Robinson handles it with striking success.
It can be studied at best advantage in *Tasker Norcross*.

The man, named Ferguson, who tells the story, has a
weird and troubling personality.   He hardly lets his
interlocutor (who may be the poet or any man representing the common lot) foist in a word, and wears a
haggard appearance.   There is a strangeness in his way
of thinking and a bluntness in his speech, half laughable,
half disquieting.   He awes his hearer into silence:

> You have an overgrown alacrity
> For saying nothing much and hearing less. . . .

We learn about the surroundings of Norcross's life.   He
lives in a goodly house.   He is well-to-do, liberal of his
money; yet there is something about him that keeps
away happiness or even a moderate share of satisfac-
tion.   He lives—or lived, for he may be dead for aught
we know—but his life is a blank.   His neighbors hardly
know him.   When asked about the man, they answered
they had nothing to say,

> And then, if they perceived a cat, they might
> Or might not have remembered what they said.
> The cat might have a personality—
> And maybe the same one the Lord left out
> Of Tasker Norcross.

The bane of Norcross was that, having no soul, he was
conscious of his want.   Was it a case of split personality,
one man in him, the dolt, being watched by the other

man, the keen-sighted guardian? Or had he been endowed in former years with normal faculties and has he lost them, while retaining the stinging sense of the loss? We are not told. But the man knew and suffered cruelly from what he knew. Ferguson comments in his philosophical, humorous way:

> Blessed are they
> That see themselves for what they never were
> Or were to be, and are, for their defect,
> At ease with mirrors and the dim remarks
> That pass their tranquil ears.

He insists on the strange duality of the man, deficient in the higher mental attributes, and aware of his deficiency. He says it in the tone of ironical banter, that more and more approaches tragic humor:

> Fasten to that
> With all the claws of your intelligence;
> And hold the man before you in his house
> As if he were a white rat in a box,
> And one that knew himself to be no other. . . .
> He would have given it all if in return
> There might have been a more sufficient face
> To greet him when he shaved.

We enter Norcross's house with Ferguson and he makes us feel palpably in what void the man moved. He was unable to find solace in reading:

> Make a slight noise
> Of recognition when you find a book

That you would not as lief read upside down
As otherwise.

The core of the man's malady lay in his inability to feel
the higher values:

He knew there was a region all around him
That lay outside man's havoc and affairs,
And yet was not all hostile to their tumult,
Where poets would have served and honored him,
And saved him, had there been anything to save.
But there was nothing. . . .

Humor of this sort skirts the realm of poetry, philosophy
and religion without losing its right to smile. It is
queerly ironical without falling short of the majesty
that belongs to high subjects. This is a feat that could
be achieved only by a writer who forced open the gates
of noble lyrical poetry, while keeping the key of the
back-door that swings in at a laughing whisper. The
contrast between the possibilities of spiritual grandeur
and the humiliating plight of the poor in spirit is powerfully set forth; yet the analyst remains self-possessed
enough to face this drama of the soul with gamesome
composure. Is Ferguson a detached observer, who gives
evidence as a witness and no more? Or does he sympa-
thise with the man and feel with him as he sees his brow
knit in anguish? If Robinson spoke in his own name,
we should be sure that his irony is the passing mood of
an idealist, who will soon turn to more comforting
thoughts. But the story is told by Ferguson, that
strange man whose eyes shone like "two cold inquiring

points of sharp metal" and seemed to wither all they fell upon.

How startling, when, reaching the conclusion, we discover, through rather entangled hints, that Ferguson and Tasker Norcross are one and the same person! Norcross was not dead in the flesh, but only in the spirit, having lost the faculty of experiencing the higher joys. He had no friend, no genius, no taste for art or poetry, no "faith larger than desperation." Those who lived in his neighborhood knew him only "as a man may know a tree." He was spiritually dead, and, horrid to say! his ghost haunted his body, grinning in its blank face, sneering at the vacant eyes, when it met them in a mirror.

The humorous poetry of Robinson, even when deeply philosophical, is not always conceived in this tragic mode. His philosophical humor can be cheerful, clad in the refined, reserved gaiety which fits his intellectual keenness and sober disposition. This is the case with *Captain Craig*.

The poem owes its name to the character whose garrulity fills page after page, in an astounding hodge-podge of all topics, in an atmosphere of now meditative, now sparkling humor. It is not a perfect composition. It somewhat lacks logical sequence and coherency. It consists of loose parts some of which might be afterthoughts. One wishes the design were more firmly drawn. There is no plot. In the refuge of a garret where Captain Craig has been housed by charitable friends, the old man talks to a little circle, of an evening, in the smoke of pipes, over a stein of beer. When the poet, who is the leading spirit of the circle, goes on a journey, he receives from Captain Craig long letters that take up the topic where the talk had left it. The temptation is great to indulge in abstract gossiping and the author does not always resist it. But it would be a mistake to discard the poem for its diluteness or occasional obscurity. It repays careful perusal. Even at the cost of skipping over a few paragraphs, one finds in it so much that is excellent—arresting characterization, mild social satire, outbursts of fun, lyrical flights, triumphant strains of philosophical poetry, in a setting of wistful humor—that one cannot but admire the wealth and strength of inspiration that presided over this strange compound of farce and wisdom.

It does not express the whole philosophy of the poet, but it voices one mood in which he is pleased for once to consider man and the universe. Robinson shows himself here a conscious artist, if not in the construction, at least in the working out of the details: he does not only prize sensuous beauty, but meditates on the part that beauty, color, the exhilaration of joy and the thrill of life, with the spiritual stimulus inherent in them, play in the general scheme of things. It is a hymn to hearty content, wholesome buoyancy and sapful liveliness. The son of the New England Puritans, here, frolicsomely breaks the fetters in which heredity and education had vainly tried to bind him. He disowns none of the elevated thoughts that habits of contemplation, practices of self-searching and the urge of spiritual aspirations had bred in him. But, through Captain Craig's humorous vagaries, he intimates that there are more truths in the world than lie in self-distrust and self-repression. His is not to vindicate the flesh in the manner Walt Whitman had done or the school of writers derived from Walt Whitman continued to do, but to broaden the outlook of the spirit by throwing down the barriers of asceticism, bigotry and cant, that had too long penned in the soul and shut it out from the splendors of nature and the gentler associations of society.

Along with the enjoyment of outward beauty grow human sympathy and love, without which social intercourse is a riot of selfish aims, religion a narrow striving towards self-centered salvation, and life a slough of despond. Although Robinson has too much tact—and sense of humor—to assume the part of preacher, one feels the poem, under its queer texture of thoughtful merriment, fraught with Christian loving kindness. Captain Craig's philosophy is a not unsuccessful attempt at reviving, by mixed touches of humor and beauty, the humane doctrine of Christ, as against the sterner teaching of the Old Testament. From another point of view, it is a plea for the spontaneous surrender to the feelings and the imagination, as against the harsh tension of the conscience or the over-exertion of the will. Although what there is of philosophy assumes at times the tone of abstract disquisition, the poet amply resorts to concrete illustration. Dreams, visions, reminiscences, stories, character-sketches, parables, symbolic scenes and mythological allusions convey the

175

thoughts in vivid pictures. There may be too many of them, nor are all equally good, but enough of them offer real interest and beauty to fill the work with exquisite poetry. Artistry, thought and humor combine to give the reader the impression of being taken away to a world of transcendent and weird reality.

The flight to the upper regions of the ideal takes place against a background of genuine humor, within sight of a ludicrous rout. Throning among them is Captain Craig, half philosopher, half merry-andrew, both pitiable and admirable, reconciling in him by some strange harmony whimsical freakishness and profound wisdom. The element of humor stands in constant contrast to the serious thought, creating striking literary effects, by sharp antitheses between the manner and the matter, riveting the reader's attention and giving freshness and novelty to the philosophical motive. The poet's power of description and characterisation, his talent for caricature, his gusto, his masterly use of apt and pithy words, his skill in coining phrases, add the beauty of expression to the quality of the conception. The poem may be of the sort that discourages perfunctory reading, but it is worthy of careful study.

Craig—captain by courtesy—would have been frowned out of the precincts of the puritan village, but that a few,

> Say five or six of us—had found somehow
> The spark in him, and we had fanned it there,
> Choked under, like a jest in Holy Writ,
> By Tilbury prudence.

176

He would have been left to starve by his righteous neighbors, too intent on maintaining the purity of the sacred fold to busy themselves about a straggler, had not the same good Samaritans provided him with a shelter and the means of keeping body and soul together for the last months of his life. For Captain Craig was old and feeble and already tottering to the grave. Yet his mind was possessed of full vigor. There was in him, so near the decline of his days, an intellectual Indian Summer that flung a glamour over his thought and made it sparkle with unusual brilliancy. Feeling that he was having his last chance of communicating his message to the world, he would inflict lengthy speeches on the charitable little group. Splendidly indifferent to poverty, illness or misfortune, he set the example of detachment from the externals of life. Not that he despised the good things of this world, but he found in his vision of higher truth a wealth of delight that no human riches could impart.

He praised the splendor of the universe, that liberally offers itself to the enjoyment of all, could they only make themselves worthy of the goodly heritage. A single beam of the sunset, caught from the pallet where he lay, was enough to attune his heart to perennial gladness. By delighting in God-created beauty, he thought man pleases the Most High better than by mechanical and selfish prayer, or by blighting life with precise ordinances and rancorous exclusions. God is not the spiteful Being that mean minds picture to themselves, belittling Him to their own image.

177

I turned a little furrow of my own
Once on a time, and everybody laughed—
As I laughed afterwards; and I doubt not
The First Intelligence, which we have drawn
In our competitive humility
As if it went forever on two legs,
Had some diversion of it: I believe
God's humor is the music of the spheres. . . .

Before creeds existed, with their gloomy fiats and blasting threats, the sun shone and God was throned on high in blissful serenity. The radiancy of dawn and eve and the glad repose of God will outlast narrow religions and surly philosophies:

You quiver and you clutch
For something larger, something unfulfilled,
Some wiser kind of joy that you shall have
Never, until you learn to laugh with God.

The poet drinks in the old wiseacre's words. But the unphilosophical friends, bewildered by the audacity of the thoughts, ruffled by the authoritative tone of the prophet, doubtful about the significance of "this tuneful ooze of rhetoric," leave, one after the other, running away from what they deem the empty ranting of a dotard. In the evening, at the club, they banter the too patient listener for his foolish forbearance and call him names:

Like "Bellows-mender to Prince Æolus,"
"Pipe-filler to the Hoboscholiast,"

"Bread-fruit for the Non-Doing," with one more
That I remember, and a dozen more
That I forget.

Yet the disciple sits at the feet of the modern Socrates, day after day. He revolves in his mind Captain Craig's teaching and feels regenerated by its marvellous appeal, as poets and mystics do when they are taken back by the strength of their new faith to their childhood and the days of immediate and perfect communion with the spirit-world.

I felt at length as one who throws himself
Down restless on a couch when clouds are dark,
And shuts his eyes to find, when he wakes up
And opens them again, what seems at first
An unfamiliar sunlight in his room
And in his life—as if the child in him
Had laughed and let him see; and then I knew
Some prowling superfluity of child
In me had found the child in Captain Craig
And let the sunlight reach him.

Those who have not enough spiritual vitality to keep the child strong in them will fall into the hopeless distemper that ailed the sombre man described by Craig, who, incapable of love or sympathy, went through life in despair.

And he would have this life no fairer thing
Than a certain time for numerous marionettes
To do the Dance of Death. Give him a rose,
And he would tell you it is very sweet,

But only for a day.   Most wonderful!
Show him a child, or anything that laughs,
And he begins at once to crunch his wormwood
And then runs on with his "realities."
What does he know about realities? . . .

Thus Robinson, following the lead of his humorous
guide, meets halfway the least jocose of poets, the
Wordsworth of *Intimations of Immortality* and the
Shelley of *Intellectual Beauty,* when they reverted to
their childhood days to discover in their subliminal consciousness a distinct intuition of the supernal world and
a feeling of the soul floating free in the illimited spaces
of pure ether.

All this is serious thought—so serious that none is
more weighty in the revelation of seers and the proph-
ecies of founders of religions.   Yet it is uttered by a beg-
gar that might have donned the motley of Shakespeare's
fools.   It is philosophical truth steeped in humor.
Even when Craig vaticinates as from the top of the
sacred mount, in the glow of the flaming bush, we remember the withered face, the enigmatic smile, the
jug of beer on the rickety table, the "patched and un-
washed attic-window," all the appurtenances of the
Bohemian environment which are part and parcel of
his personality.   And his talk, as is natural, periodically
relapses into the burlesque.   Note in what terms he
asseverates his faith in future life and salvation:

Though I look back through barren years enough
To make me seem—as I transmute myself
In downward retrospect from what I am—

As unproductive and as unconvinced
Of living bread and the soul's eternal draught
As a frog on a Passover-cake in a streamless desert,—
Still do I trust the light that I have earned,
And having earned, received.   You shake your head,
But do not say that you will shake it off.

By a feat of spiritual conjuring, humor becomes the vehicle of thought.   It becomes also the effective instrument of pathos, for Captain Craig is old and near his end, and he knows it.   The classical lore that he picked up while rambling through devious ways provides him with mythological imagery to intimate his forebodings of approaching death.   The passage is as beautiful and moving as a stanza of Keats, clothed in tragedy and splendor, with a touch of the "familiar sublime."

                              Halfway back
I made a mild allusion to the Fates,
Not knowing then that ever I should have
Dream-visions of them, painted on the air,—
Clotho, Lachesis, Atropos.   Faint-hued
They seem, but with a faintness never fading,
Unblurred by gloom, unshattered by the sun,
Still with eternal color, colorless,
They move and they remain.   The while I write
These very words I see them,—Atropos,
Lachesis, Clotho; and the last is laughing.
When Clotho laughs, Atropos rattles her shears;
But Clotho keeps on laughing just the same.
Some time when I have dreamed that Atropos
Has laughed, I'll tell you how the colors change—
The colors that are changeless, colorless. . . .

Such an admirable renewal of mythological poetry, full of mingled grace and majesty, of pathos and serenity, of classical poise and romantic glamour, of lyrical sweetness and homely harmony, reveals the great master. We condone a few failings of lengthiness or obscurity when we are given such splendid compensation.

In the shadow of death, Captain Craig bequeaths to the world his gospel of love and mercy. To those who have let ignoble scrambling for material wealth, or sour resentment for trifling offenses, or harsh intolerance, smother in them the gentler inclinations, he recalls the true doctrine of Christ, too often neglected by men and women who go by the name of Christians. He does it without naming the master, through a parable, which is the record of a dream. The allusion is clear. The mystery that surrounds it enhances its beauty. He relates that he went to sleep haunted by the thought of making his wretched life useful. He was a carpenter, lying in the shade of a cedar tree with his tools by his side. The tools were dull, useless for building the new house, and he felt the horrible temptation to hack out his life with them—when he heard a soft tread coming in his direction. The august visitor engaged in a conversation with him, and what he said was meant for all ears. He wound up:

"But are you sure," he asked, "that you have skill?
And are you sure that you have learned your trade?
No, you are not."—He looked at me and laughed
As he said that; but I did not laugh then,
Although I might have laughed.— "They are dull," said he,

"They were not very sharp if they were ground;
But they are what you have, and they will earn
What you have not.   So take them as they are,
Grind them and clean them, put new handles to them,
And then go learn your trade in Nazareth."

A few moments before he gasped his last, Craig faltered
the ultimate warning:

Forget you not that he who in his work
Would mount from these low roads of measured shame
To tread the leagueless highway must fling first,
And fling forevermore beyond his reach
The shackles of a slave who doubts the sun.
There is no servitude so fraudulent
As of a sun-shut mind. . . .

Thus passed away Captain Craig, a humorist who had
more wisdom in him and spoke more truth than many
a capped and gowned don mouthing sanctimonious
homilies.   Although the poem is not perfect, it keeps
up in most of its parts the difficult alliance of serious
purpose and humorous characterisation.   Robinson
happily resisted the temptation to make humor the
vehicle of sarcasm or satire, as Swift had done in his contempt for mankind or Carlyle in his bitter indignation
at the ways of the world.   The poison of pessimism
is absent from his poems.   When his inspiration wraps
itself in darkness, it is the darkness of tragedy, not that
of despondency or despair.

We must remember the fundamentally idealistic trend
of his poetry when we approach the last two pieces we

183

shall deal with in this study, one referring to Napoleon in the last phase, the other to Rembrandt at the tragic turning of his career. A less catholic writer would have avoided such sombre subjects. But Robinson's optimism is of no cheap quality. It is not that of Pangloss, who makes a mess of life by ignoring evil. It is rather that of Candide, who faces evil manfully in order to foil it by sustained effort, or, if the forces of fatality are too strong, to bear it with resignation. Yet, resignation is the virtue of which Napoleon is least capable. That is why, near his end, when all hope is lost, he gives the sorry spectacle of a man carried away by frantic passion to delirium. He is pilloried by the poet in the wild attitude of the frenzied loser at the game of chance, maddened to be penned on a sea-girt rock, while the wide world, which he purposed to conquer, settles to forgetting his baneful empire. The Rembrandt poem, on the contrary, in spite of the bitter irony aimed at the stupidity of the philistines, shows the master bravely rallying in adversity, under circumstances in which others would have sunk in weariness or cowardly given up the struggle. Both poems belong to the kind that may be called "grim humor."

Napoleon is raving in one of the fits of semi-madness which hardly leave him since he has been thrown helpless by his victorious foes on the island of St. Helena. What a situation for the conqueror of the world! He, who battled with the armies of Europe, is reduced now to wage a mean fight against the vermin that infest his cabin.

184

Ha! Look you, there's a rat.
Last night there were a dozen on that shelf,
And two of them were living in my hat.

He, who rose elate to the pinnacle whence he commanded Victory and basked in the sun of Marengo and Austerlitz, paces now on a low strand at the foot of a rock, drenched by continuous rain.

For said the Lord: Imprimis, we have rats,
And having rats, we have rain.—
So on the seventh day
He rested, and made Pain.

What wonder that his brain has grown distracted! Like Lear's, in his distress, his speech strays from sound reason; but there is sense in his wild utterances, the sense that all is lost and that an awful grief is gnawing at his heart. The rats may be there, tripping on the floor and fretting the rim of his hat, but they are more surely within his breast making a red feast of his vitals. The ignoble physical image becomes a horrid symbol of his mental agony.

He is too proud to complain. The time is past for rhetoric. The stage on which he strutted a few glittering hours has crumbled to ruins; there is not even one plank of it left from which he might hurl bigmouthed denunciation at his tormentors. There remains only sarcasm, the weapon of the vanquished, whose blows, powerless against unreachable enemies, return home and gash his bosom with bitter bloodless wounds.   This is the source of ghastly humor, which the poet wields with tragic effectiveness.

The defeated emperor serves his time of expiation in the setting that is most abhorrent to him.   Everywhere about him the sea, where the English resisted his on-slaught, and where he is imprisoned now, on a speck of land, surrounded by the waste of waters.   Its mighty rumor

> Fades and swells and overflows
> Like music underneath and overhead,

and joins in maddening accord with the feverish buzz that beats his brain from within.   His rage helplessly fizzles out in sneers.

> What lowering outland hostelry is this
> For one the stars have disinherited? . . .
> An acreage of God's forgetfulness
> Left here above the foam and long ago
> Made right for my duress.

We feel the breath hissing between his clenched teeth as his laden soul disburdens itself in deepest irony. Every word, with its imaginative coloring, and its taunt-ing stateliness, as shreds of imperial majesty still cling-ing about the wreck of lost power, deals out relentless self-mockery.

Visions of his past flit across his ken, most vivid of all the remembrance of that ominous morning on the plain of Waterloo

When Fate, the mistress of iniquities,
The mad Queen-spinner of all discrepancies,
Beguiled the dyers of the dawn that day,
And even in such a curst and sodden way
Made my three colors one.

His it is not to feel disturbed with self-reproach or to writhe under pangs of remorse. When the thought of slaughtered men and dying wails on bleak battlefields crosses his brain, he discards it with flippant unconcern,

A thousand here and there may shriek and freeze,
Or they may starve in fine.
The Old Physician has a crimson cure
For such as these.

His only interest is in himself, in the cruel downfall of his hopes, in the biting sense of ruin. He feels incensed at Fate, the jilting hag, at his Daemon, the traitor, that "has ruined the last chorus of the play." His distracted brain begets fearful ghosts, that project themselves outside, and stalk derisively before his gaze, strewing rotten laurels on his path. They become the butts of his scathing irony.

But his self-taunting pales before the irony of Fortune, which has left him stranded on his hundred-foot square of barren shore, in howling immensity, haunted by idle phantasms and distracting memories. This irony materializes in the rats and the rain, and in other startling devices, which are master-strokes of tragic humor. Napoleon is pursued by snatches of the old French song,

in which the populace of the time of Louis XIV had
ridiculed the Duke of Marlborough.   The funny burden
of it: *Mironton, mironton, mirontaine,* bursts out like
an uncanny peal of laughter in the midst of a funeral.
And the fallen emperor is not alone: he has one companion, an English doctor, who persistently presses him
to take medicine.   The comic resentment of the ex-
asperated patient sets the final touch to the lugubrious
farce.

> Man, I could murder you almost,
> You with your pills and toast.
> Take it away and eat it, and shoot rats . . .
> You say that I'll achieve it if I try?
> Swallow it?—No, not I—
> God, what a way to die!

Rembrandt, at the painful moment of an artist's life
when he sees public favor slipping away from him, remains an artist, that is, a man of fine intelligence and
noble feelings, who does not let himself go to violent
words or unseemly behavior.   He judges severely, as he
is entitled to, the imbecility of his countrymen, who,
unable to appreciate the subtle play of lights and
shadows of his late manner, reproach him with not giving them solid portraits with plain likeness.   His irony
is trenchant, as well it may, but with a reserve, a self-
control, a fortitude of thought, which show the superior
character and the great genius.   Robinson, as a humorist, calls into activity the faculty of psychological analysis, which gives such finesse and lifelike truthfulness to

his narrative and interpretative poems. Here, the
humor is rich in psychological values, delicately brought
out through the froth of raillery. Rembrandt speaks
to himself:

> Observe yourself as you discern yourself
> In your discredited ascendency. . . .
> For there are shadows and obscurities
> Immediate or impending on your view,
> That may be worse than you have ever painted
> For the bewildered and unhappy scorn
> Of injured Hollanders in Amsterdam
> Who cannot find their fifty florins' worth
> Of Holland face where you have hidden it
> In your new golden shadow. . . .

Since the thick-witted burgesses do not understand any
other portrait-painting than the display of rose-colored
flesh in crude light, they look upon Rembrandt's subtle
chiaroscuro as the sign of a distracted mind. The
painter remarks ironically:

> And here's a fellow painting in the dark—
> A loon who cannot see that he is dead
> Before God lets him die. He paints away
> At the impossible, so Holland has it,
> For venom or for spite, or for defection,
> Or else for God knows what. Well, if God knows,
> And Rembrandt knows, it matters not so much
> What Holland knows or cares. If Holland wants
> Its heads all in a row, and all alike,
> There's Franz to do them and to do them well . . .
> And one as like a rabbit as another.

Disgusted with the blockheads, Rembrandt turns to his familiar sprite, who, assuming the tone of philosophical detachment speaks flippantly, intimating that success and fame will not count so much when he is in the grave:

> What if in fifty or a hundred years
> They find you out? You may have gone meanwhile
> So greatly to the dogs that you'll not care
> Much what they find. If this be all you are—
> This unaccountable aspiring insect—
> You'll sleep as easy in oblivion
> As any sacred monk or parricide;
> And if, as you conceive, you are eternal,
> Your soul may laugh, remembering (if a soul
> Remembers) your befrenzied aspiration
> To smear with certain ochres and some oil
> A few more perishable ells of cloth.

There is no more pathetic humor than this uncrowning of a great man's glory by bringing him down to the common measure of the dust we all return to. Even a peerless genius must be invaded at times by the dismal thought of mortality and smile sardonically at the vision of the lurid corpse overcome by the conquering worm. Robinson's power of expression gives to this notion an arresting force of individuality and striking aptness to the personage and situation. But Rembrandt is sure of himself and of his genius. His aim is not to reach present success, but to pursue ideal beauty. There are other subjects for painting than the smug-faced citizens who grin at their pictures when they are done. He will enlarge the field of pictorial art and render the glow of color and the shimmering of light that transmute the meanest objects, were it sliced beef at a butcher's stall. Addressing himself to his new task with grim energy, Rembrandt gives up any lingering desire for void applause, near or remote:

> If at the first
> Of your long turning, which may still be longer
> Than even your faith has measured it, you sigh
> For distant welcome that may not be seen,
> Or wayside shouting that will not be heard,
> You may as well accommodate your greatness
> To the convenience of an easy ditch,
> And, anchored there with all your widowed gold,
> Forget your darkness in the dark, and hear
> No longer the cold wash of Holland scorn.

This is the last of his wavering; the very bitterness of his laugh has braced him to brave striving. Humor is the defensive-offensive weapon which the giant wields to rout the swarm of pigmies that would have silenced his genius under their croaking, had he doubted his own strength. The rich intellectuality of the poem gives significance to its humor and its humor sets off the deep meaning of the intellectuality.

Robinson's humor is not a mere outburst of mirth with eddies of laughter and sparks of wit twinkling at the surface. It is part of the woof and warp of the poems, an organic element of the texture of the scenes and narratives, incorporated to the characters and intimately blended with the essence of the themes. It

191

is as distinctly fraught with thought as the psychological analysis and the moral interpretation. It is a sign of intellectual breadth; for the reality of the spirit is as complex as the myriad-faced aspects of the world. Robinson encompasses the whole realm of the mind, from the plain facts that stand in the foreground to the subtle intimations that lurk in the mysterious haze of thoughtful humor. He seizes the flexible outlines, the moving relations, the variegated coloring, the winking shadows, all that gives saliency, warmth and lifelikeness to the spiritual landscape. Humor is one of the most meaning ways at his disposal to bring out the vivid contrasts or fleeting oppositions whereby literature can best express the ceaseless welter of waves of thought meeting waves of feeling, instinct clashing against will, individual whim encountering social discipline, desire grappling with experience, genius battered by mediocrity, wisdom struggling against prejudice, hope overcome by fate. Robinson's humor beats with the pulse of life. Where narration would be cold or tragedy too massive, humor adapts itself to the windings of sinuous thought or serpentine feeling. It deals with minor conflicts, venial faults, lesser ridicules or skin-deep sentiments in a light vein that rouses a smile without excluding sympathy. It admits of gentle criticism tempered by kindness. It can also adapt itself to the compelling touch of the poet versed in the deeper truths of the human heart and rise to the summit of emotion. It can be freighted with wisdom and pathos. But its tragic hues are seldom unmixed with more cheerful tints; they generally move against a background of comforting idealism. Even when Robinson's humor skirts the boundary of madness, there is in its grimness a leaven of vitality and a mental vigor that saves the rights of the spirit and creates wonder at the strength of mind battling against destiny.

Robinson shows a wide range in his treatment of humor. At his best he obtains a perfect fusion of the apparently discordant elements that enter into its making. How does he achieve the conciliation of those opposites? It is the secret of his genius. We must give up the method of logical disquisition regarding this mystery of his art. But there is one thing we may assert with certainty: as in the case of his lyrical, epic or interpretative poetry, the essence of his humor—its charm, gaiety, winsomeness, strength of appeal, pathos and vital truth—lies in the poet's genuine, thoughtful and catholic humanity.

CHAPTER VI

PSYCHOLOGY

ROBINSON'S natural gifts of observation and sympathy, and his experience of human nature, acquired through keen insight into behavior and motives and through grave contemplation, make him a master of psychological analysis. This field attracted him from the beginning of his career, as a means to detach himself from the *ego* and treat objectively themes of broad human import. On entering this path, he consciously broke away from the romantic trend, which our age has fairly outgrown, and sought in character-painting and in dramatic narrative (sometimes interspersed with thoughtful humor) new sources of literary interest and of poetical emotion. In this he is in agreement with the chief tendency of our generation, which is above all eager to know truth and derives more pleasure from an imaginative rendering of the actualities of the human heart than from fantastic vagaries or sentimental effusions. At any rate, admitting there may still be room for constructions of airy splendor, flights of the spirit towards the absolute or outpourings of wild individual passion, the stronger current is in the direction of a realistic presentation of the world—either the outer world of social relations or the inner world of thought

194

and feeling. Why should not poetry take the hint from this change of taste, which is an unmistakable sign of a new attitude towards life? Classic poetry had made of man's mind and heart the proper object of its study, and raised the conflict of will against passion to epic grandeur or dramatic intensity. The progress of science in our time and the activities of psychological research have made us eager to go further in the scrutiny of mental life. We are not satisfied with the plain presentation of manifest behavior or of obvious motives; we find keen intellectual pleasure in dim shades of feelings and remote workings of the mind. Literature has made psychology its favorite auxiliary. It rested with poetry to show that exact knowledge of subtle truths is not incompatible with the creation of beauty.

Browning first ventured on the ground of psychological observation with the set purpose of reaping, from it, materials for tense descriptions and pathetic monologues heightened by rhythmical and imaginative expression. He not only inaugurated a new *genre,* but explored a vast tract of the mind's precincts, and created a forcible and original style to suit his novel poetical inspiration. He is unequalled in his range of intellectual activity and his vigor of psychological acumen. He will probably remain long the master of intellectual poetry. But he did not exhaust the possibilities of treating the facts of the mind as a new source of the energies or harmonies of song. Robinson, a follower and disciple of Browning, developed his own conception of truth, beauty and pathos, and, belonging to a later generation, profited by the discoveries of the science of the mind, carried in our time to deeper layers of phenomena and more elusive elements of the psychic reality.

The most significant advance of psychology in the XXth century has been in the domain of the subconscious. Recent investigations have established beyond doubt that there exists under the surface of clear apprehension a deeper current of intuitions and incipient feelings that exert a covert influence on our determinations. In dreamy, mystical, impulsive natures, these obscure suggestions play even a greater part than the definite acts of the will, and, when properly interpreted, give the key to apparently sudden decisions, that had, in fact, been long brewing in the twilight of the subliminal self. In minds trained to the exercise of reason, the subconscious may also be the seat of dark broodings, that, when they emerge into light, possess a surprising power to hasten or retard deliberate action. Those dark mental processes, whether they remain impenetrable to the subject himself, or reveal themselves in lightning flashes of retrospective illumination, offer to the observer, if endowed with a fair gift of divination, a store of precious knowledge, and to the poet, if favored with sympathetic insight and the power of dramatic construction, treasures of rich potentialities. How many whimsical, inconsistent or burlesque characters may thus become intelligible! How many cases of unexplained melancholy or strange decline may thus yield

196

their secret! How many tragedies of the soul may thus be discovered under an outward appearance of composure or of conventional decorum! How many sudden resolutions, or, in extreme cases, criminal acts or suicides may thus be accounted for!

This is one of the sources from which Robinson draws the lineaments of some of his most arresting stories or dramatic monologues. His power of artistic creation so well succeeds in blending the soul-ingredients with the concrete details of the action, and in integrating the subtle mental experiences to the human interest, that there appears no trace of effort. There lies about the finished work an intellectual quality, due to its very connection with the less accessible elements of the mind, which adds to it a penetrating vigor and irresistible immediacy.

The atmosphere of the subconscious is permeated with mystery. It embraces an order of strange facts, which bear the dual character of indisputable reality and of elusive remoteness. Robinson, a symphonist of soul-values, assembles the overtones and the undertones that lie dormant in the cells of the affective or conceptual memory, and wraps them in waves of weird spiritual harmony. He needs not, like the romantic poets, conjure from the realm of the unreal "the light that never was on sea or land"; he has only to follow the guidance of his sensibility and trust his knowledge of the finer vibrations of the mind, to achieve the supreme feat of poetry—the evocation of wonder. He weaves around us a net of revelations and surprises, wins us over to his

vision, and gently leads us to a state of delighted bewilderment. By such effects, poetry fulfils its true
mission, which is to carry us away, on golden waves of
song or in a storm of frowning splendor, to a place of
vantage, whence we discover appeasing or appalling
sights that the dullness of our minds had shut out from
our view. Sober thoughtfulness or tragic sombreness
are moods to which Robinson is often led by his meditative genius, intent on wrenching from life its most significant secrets. The triumph of his art, in his psychological narratives, is the handling of pathos through the
medium of pensive mystery.

Such poetry voices the spirit of an advanced civilization, which, having freed man from the grosser preoccu-
pations of material life, gives full scope to the complex
activities of the intellect and the sensibility. Refinement, acquired by the accelerated play of the higher
faculties, is not an unmixed boon. It brings along with
it a mental strain, which, in some cases, results in over-
fatigue or exhaustion. All brains are not strong enough
to stand the impact of the ever-renewed appeal of tense
sensations or emotions. Some collapse and sink to a
state of mental inertia, where all that gives price to
life seems to vanish out of reach. Others are stung to
over-sensitiveness and fret in feverish anxiety at the
least excitation. The bane of our time (perhaps more
in America than anywhere else) is neurotic hyperes-
thesia, which culminates in restless agitation and may
end in nervous break-down. Robinson is keenly alive
to the possibilities which pathological psychology opens

to the painter of characters or the teller of dramatic tales. He has explored this field, not in search of cheap horrors, but with a sure sense of the relations of the abnormal to the normal, the former being often the emphatic demonstration of what morbidity may lurk in the state of unstable mental equilibrium which is not infrequent in our time. In his dramatic presentation of disordered minds he is careful to choose the state of disintegration which preserves enough of the balance of sanity to excite our sympathy, and yet to raise about the case a chiaroscuro of mysterious strangeness. Some of his most arresting characters, like the greatest Shakespearian figures, totter on the verge of madness, near enough the abyss to make us shudder, yet keeping that shaky firmness of tread which saves the night-walker from immediate destruction.

Robinson thus creates a new psychological realism made up of precise observation and of imaginative vision, which belongs to the literary *genre* inaugurated by Browning, yet preserves a distinct and striking mark of originality. The subconscious and the pathological provide him with motives of heightened human significance; or he describes normal minds in a state of excitement, under the pressure of strong passions, at a crisis of their lives where the deeper forces of the personality assume unwonted energy or clash in heart-stirring conflict.

In his first collection of verse, *The Children of the Night,* made up of short poems written before he was thirty, the subjective element is not quite fused yet into

199

the broader, more detached view of life which he was to take later. Yet psychological analysis is already at work, with some of the qualities of finesse, penetration, novelty and dramatic instancy, which were to become the very tincture of his genius.

In three lightly tripping stanzas, he expresses his regret at not having discovered the true worth of a friend "until he died." This is as the title indicates an "Old Story," but there is no triteness in the reasons to which he attributes his blindness. The psychologist ruthlessly applies the vivisector's knife on himself:

> I cursed him for the ways he had
> To make me see
> My envy of the praise he had
> For praising me.

He is already fond of character-drawing. He has not yet the large experience or the probing keenness that will give him later a sure grasp of the complex causes of human actions; but the suddenness and unexpectedness of his dénouements presuppose the divination of the deeper secrets of the conscience. His sketches are contained in a sonnet, or in a group of quatrains, so dense with compact thought and feeling that they seem as full as a ripe fruit. They often wind up with a thrilling conclusion—a sudden act of despair, an unaccountable flight, a suicide—which reveals some sore spot in the man's bosom, under the outer crust of coarseness or blithe courtesy.

The treatment of love is a sure test to sound a poet's

temper. Robinson's work contains few love lyrics; his best ones occur in his recent work, the *Tristram*. At the age when young poets overflow with bubbling sentiment, he was shy of romantic themes. It is not in his youthful years, at the period of life when almost every man's tongue gets vocal with heart-songs, that love became one of his leading motives. Later only, after he had made the final choice of the objective manner, did love-poems appear among his compositions, often with the warmth that reveals sincere emotion and deep reverence for the passion of passions, but above all with a wealth of psychological knowledge which places them (even if they happen to fail in sweetness) above the ordinary range of love poetry.

His Arthurian poems are the richest in poetical and dramatic love-values, mostly dependent for their charm or pith on the truth of the psychological notations. We have already shown the deep humanity of the characters and the lifelikeness of the drama. We must insist upon the shadings in the soul-picture that differentiate the poems. They are poems in which love plays a great or a prominent part, presenting a pathetic ebb and flow of feelings, from the bliss of mutual tenderness to the sorrow of estrangement and separation, based (in two of them) on the contrast between the instability of the man's passion and the trust of the woman in the duration of plighted love. But how different the acting characters, according to their temper, station, ways of life and the circumstances in which they are involved! We leave aside Merlin, Lancelot, Tristram, the aged sage, the impetuous knight, the introspective minstrel whose idiosyncrasies are so plainly opposed. We shall confine our attention to Vivian, Guinevere and Isolt, and try to show what striking individuality the poet gave to each of them, by sheer delicacy of psychological delineation. All three are endowed with an unusual power of seduction and personify the forces of sentiment. But they stand as far apart, in spite of some similarity in the situations, as Spenser's Acrasia, Shakespeare's Cleopatra and Sidney's Stella.

Vivian, entrancingly pretty and selfish, was enjoying tranquilly the delights of her fairy-palace and of self-contemplation before the arrival of Merlin, waiting without impatience for the expected completion of her happiness. There was to be as much glad surprise and pride, as fond attachment, in her love. The care of her green arbor, the decoration of her purple bower, the designing of her dresses and the choice of her jewels were enough to satisfy her, although not to suppress the vague wish to conquer the unconquerable maker of kings and builder of empires. Her temper is made up of a blending of tenderness and irony; her mood is that of playful sweetness; her love is all compact of intellectual sprightliness. She enjoys subduing the rugged gruffness of the unkempt sage as a child circling the neck of a mastiff with a silk braid. What an impish pleasure she takes in having Blaise reap the wizard's beard and change his sable robe for a garment "of purple, touched with gold, and fledged with snowy lace"! With what light merriment she descants on the metamorphosis of the tamed philosopher, with mixed mockery and fancifulness!

> Since I have had your name
> To dream of and say over to myself,
> The visitations of that awful beard
> Have been a terror for my nights and days—
> . . . I've seen it like an ocean,
> Blown seven ways at once and wrecking ships . . .
> I've seen it woven into shining ladders
> That ran up out of sight and so to heaven,
> All covered with white ghosts with hanging robes
> Like folded wings . . .

She is witty as a Greek hetaira of Lucian's and demure as a mediaeval maiden of Chrestien de Troyes'. She has all the seductive wile of Tasso's Armida, with the reserve of an earth-treading madonna. There is beauty and grace in her modest behavior, as when she received Merlin in the "flame-shaken gloom" of her hall, or pledged him with a cup of golden wine and

> smiled at him across their gleaming rims,
> From eyes that made a fuel of the night,
> . . . and shot glory over gold
> At Merlin, while their cups touched and his trembled.

At other times the passionate flame contained in her bosom will issue forth from the depths of the subconscious. The bandying of clever repartees ceases; the challenge of playful taunts hangs in suspense; she feels in the grip of an imperious force, which she yields to and, at the same time, wields as a powerful weapon:

. . . and with hot lips that left
The world with only one philosophy
For Merlin or for Anaxagoras,
Called his to meet them and in one long hush
Of rapture to surrender . . .

She is not above jealousy or free from fear that the precious happiness, secured after so long waiting and scheming, may escape her. But she is not enough of the languorous lover for her heart to writhe in anguish. It is in a tone of mild banter at Merlin and at herself that she alludes to a possible waning of his love. She will not, she says, be constantly buzzing at his ears like an inopportune bee, lest he should, with an impatient stroke of his hand, carelessly smite her life away. But, in spite of the unobtrusiveness of her affection and the brilliancy of her wit, the time comes when Merlin feels his destiny so entangled with the fate of King Arthur's kingdom, that he must break off the sweet tie. She feels a change creeping over their amorous relations—too intelligent not to see his growing coldness, and too wise, in her thoughtful light-heartedness, not to prepare herself for the inevitable reversion. The separation is brusque, rapid, cutting short all recriminations and reproaches. The episode winds up, leaving us under no deep concern, as we feel Vivian will find new interests in life, whether she entraps new lovers in her gins or enjoys the companionship of her own sweet self.

Not so with Guinevere in the *Lancelot*. Passing from one poem to the other is moving from gentle emotions ruffling the surface of our mind with beauteous melancholy fancies, to a soul-stirring tragedy. Guinevere is a type of *grande amoureuse,* a passionate lover who staked her whole being on the distracting adventure of her guilty liaison, and will live or die of it. The atmosphere of the poem is colored with glaring hues of intense passion in an impressive harmony of sombre tints and pathetic strokes. The wild jealousy and bloody anger of King Arthur, the sad earnestness of Lancelot weary of criminal dissembling and irresistibly urged by his better self to seek the Light, the desperate frenzy of the Queen struggling against her doom and blindly clinging to her last shreds of happiness, form a compact whole built with the solidity of great Elizabethan drama. The psychology of the characters— above all, that of the Queen on the slippery slope to her undoing—develops with the inner logic and the deep human truth that we observe in Shakespeare, unless it be also in Racine. The crisis culminates in the separation scene, which becomes, as befits the thoughtful structure of the plot, an abstract of the whole psychological structure. Guinevere's utterances sound now like the pleadings of Cleopatra, now like the ravings of Phèdre. Enraged at Lancelot's fatal magnanimity, who obtained Arthur's forgiveness and opened to her, as he thought, the calm of appeased feelings, she frantically cavils at his well-meant words, perversely keeping up the fiction of their dead love. He had, in melancholy retrospect, alluded to the past glamour of their days, that were *then* so glorious. She bursts out:

Why do you stab me now
With such a needless "then"? If I am going—
And I suppose I am—are the words all lost
That men have said before to dogs and children
To make them go away? Why use a knife,
When there are words enough without your *then*
To cut as deep as need be?

She clutches like a drowning woman at the least straw
she fancies may support her:

Am I so old
And dull, so lean and waning, or what not,
That you must hurry away to grasp and hoard
The small effect of time I might have stolen
From you and from a Light that where it lives
Must live forever?

She tremblingly points to a possible issue where there
might be a dim ray of hope left for her:

Why must I go
To Camelot when your kinsmen hold all France?
Why is there not some nook in some old house
Where I might hide myself—with you or not?

She loses all sense of measure and pitiably seeks to
appropriate the power of dispensing supreme justice:

If I were God,
I should say, "Let them be as they have been.
A few more years will heap no vast account
Against eternity, and all their love
Was what I gave them" . . .

Having thus passed through the pathetic phases of love's agony—fury, reproach, imploring, frantic imagining—there remains only the last move that will bring her forgetfulness and some measure of rest in the death-like solitude of Almesbury.

Isolt has a passionate fervor in her, burning like a steady flame, not leaping out in angry spurts of revolt against necessity. The situation in which she finds herself is very different from that which maddens Guinevere into rage and furious struggle. Yet the two characters diverge from each other mostly because of the individuality of their constitutions. Love with Isolt, prompt to manifest itself in fond demonstrations, is essentially of a poetical and ideal quality. Her sensibility and imagination grow so thrillingly alive that to her view the world dissolves into a floating mist, where nothing but love remains, bright with the glow of its own intensity. She feeds on elevated thoughts and sublimated feelings which make everything immaterial —the past overshadowed by grief, the present unsettled by threat of danger, the future melting into dread uncertainty, fate frowning from the clouds, death lurking in darkness like a furtive phantom.

> Before we die,
> Tell me how many lives ago it was
> I left you in the moonlight on those stairs,
> And for God's reason then did not go mad!
> Tell me how old the world was when it died—
> For I have been alone with time so long
> That time and I are strangers.

The world, fluid like a dream, assumes an impalpable beauty, which, diffusing itself in boundless space, wraps all things in the glamour of infinity.

> Leave me the stars
> A little longer, said Isolt. In Cornwall,
> So much alone there with them as I was,
> One sees into their language and their story.
> They must be more than fire; and if the stars
> Are more than fire, what else is there for them
> To be than love?

Thus, superterrestrial aspiration, tenderness beyond the reach of ordinary human nature, idealism akin to the divine, unite to raise Isolt's love to an exalted pitch, when, for rare moments, she conquers her fear of sinister omens. Soon fate looms up again and bars the horizon. Isolt then shows touching patience and resignation. The only thing she wishes for is that she alone may be offered as a victim to the Destinies, and Tristram may live to achieve great deeds and remember her, even if another woman should take possession of his heart.

> Do not forget, my love, that once Isolt
> Said that; and wheresoever she may be then,
> See her where she is now—alone with you,
> And willing enough to be alone in heaven—
> Or hell, if so it be—and let you live
> Down here without her for a thousand years,
> Were that the way of happiness for you.

Her love attains the highest form that love can reach, since it is not only the gift of heart and self, but the sacrifice of life, to keep the beloved out of harm's way.

Roman Bartholow, a novel in verse, takes us away from "storied legend" to an episode of contemporary life, where the central character is a woman, driven by trying circumstances through a grievous ordeal of sorrow and despair. Here again psychological truth is the main feature, and a keen analysis of the feelings the chief interest. The process of soul-searching is, indeed, so minute and laborious, that the intellectual effort required to follow it exceeds sometimes the capacity of the casual reader, although the happy use of images to express facts of the mind dots the compact pages with many bright spots and there are humorous digressions, often of felicitous effect. A serious fault resides in the characters: the three of them—husband, wife and friend—are insufficiently differentiated and practice self-scrutiny or philosophical hair-splitting rather in the author's manner, than according to the logic of their temper. Yet, in spite of too many long drawn out speeches, over-subtle developments and somewhat artificial dialogues, the psychological data are so firmly conceived and rendered that a study of the poem compensates the pains it gives.

The psychological drama revolves around the person of Gabrielle. She does not rush headlong, like Guinevere, into the dangerous complexities of guilty love. She is an average middle-class American woman—not one of the restless minority that beset the divorce-courts to get a chance of making new experiments in conjugal felicity. She has the loyalty and constancy of a true life-mate—would have, rather, if she were even moderately encouraged. As things are, Bartholow, her husband, is of all men the least able to foster in her the natural womanly quality of the "clinging vine."

Who was responsible at first for the estrangement? It seems that *he* must be declared the culprit. A man of means, living in a roomy country-house amid books and the portraits of his ancestors, he had not in himself the individual resources that might have counteracted the withering effect of rural solitude. His case is one of intellectual penury and moral bluntness. He is not endowed with enough geniality to enrich his and his wife's conjugal life by a constant renewal of their affection. He has not sufficient mental alertness to broaden his cramped outlook with literary or artistic interests —still less to grace hers by any adornment of the mind or gratification of the heart. She has gradually drifted from him and taken refuge in her own thoughts—with fitful outbursts of caustic raillery. She may have been wrong in thus liberally wielding woman's defensive weapon, especially when she flouted his stiff-necked grandfather (whose portrait he so much resembles), or sneered at his Greek books (which she suspects to be above his understanding). But who would reproach her with trying to make the walls of her prison ring with occasional laughter? She was beautiful, alive and gay, and her mild fondness for harmless fun was but the warrant of the honest sincerity of her nature— yet, under this ripple of carping mirth, how much actual discouragement! What pain of the mind! What heart-bruise! And, may we conjecture: what secret unconscious yearning!

When the poem begins, Bartholow has just entered a new phase of his intellectual and sentimental existence. His friend Penn-Raven, on a visit which he was asked to prolong, has infused into him unwonted vitality. At the contact of this apparently genial good fellow, Bartholow awakes from his torpor and seems to relish the beauty of nature and the sap of life for the first time. He even discovers Gabrielle, whom he had taken as a matter of course and treated like a fixture in the house ... But Gabrielle has experienced too much disappointment to let herself be easily won over. She plies her wit at this strange revival of her husband. . . . Meanwhile, Penn-Raven, who proves a cunning dissembler, lays siege to the beautiful young wife. He slily tries to work his way into Gabrielle's good graces by gentle condolence and skilful blandishment. He has discovered the thoughtful woman in her and speaks the language that is more likely to reach her heart through her intellect.

> Will you look at me and answer?
> I am not asking much in saying that,
> For I am asking only everything—
> Which in our coin of words may more than often
> Weigh less than little.

His closer approaches gradually bespeak his amorous design.

Now sets in the soul drama for Gabrielle. She is not the woman to fly into hysterics or to play the "insulted one" in an outburst of theatrical anger. She remains calm, yet with a tremor in her thoughts that betrays the inner disturbance. May not proffered love and possible happiness, placed as she is, be worthy of regard? She receives Penn-Raven's entreaties with less indifference than appears on the outside, until, under the burden of conflicting feelings, she feels invaded by haunting melancholy.

> My life (she says) is less
> To me to-night than I may give a stranger
> Out of my purse, to keep him warm and fed
> Till he forgets me.

We gradually enter into the recesses of her soul. The heart-wounds her married life has inflicted upon her have undermined her stamina. Under the surface-sheen of jeering wit and ironical gaiety, in her lies a streak of despondency. Fleeting signs dimly point to the painful struggle that takes place in her inmost being. Her conscience does not allow her to walk the gay path of passionate indulgence. Yet she has not the strength of will to break away both from unworthy husband and guilty lover, and take refuge in proud self-sufficiency. Again, there sounds in her ear the insinuating plaint of Penn-Raven:

> Had the stranger been wiser,
> Your beauty and your nearness and your burden
> Might not have overwhelmed his loyalty,

212

Or, for a time, blotted out everything
There was for him but you—and was not you;
Though he believed it was until one day
The fire that he had let you build for him
Upon his altar suddenly went out,
And there was in his temple only smoke
And darkness.

She is not wholly insensitive to what seems sincere devotion on his part; but whatever fluttering sympathy rises in her heart is smothered in a surge of bitter self-contempt. When, one night, her husband comes into the room where she is with Penn-Raven, and guesses from her constrained countenance the meaning of the situation, but exaggerates it into a wrong she has not committed, the shame of being detected at an equivocal moment, crushes in her all courage to live. Under the sting of Bartholow's unjust accusations, she flies to a desperate resolve. The path down the lawn leads to the river; she takes it—and was never seen any more.

This lamentable fate of Gabrielle might be the sensational ending of a melodrama, if it did not rest upon truthful psychological analysis and were not the logical conclusion of protracted mental anguish. Such a subject, according to the treatment it receives, can fall below the level of art or rise to the heights of beauty. The quality of Robinson's poem lies as much in his knowledge of the human heart as in his power of dramatic construction. He never interferes to comment on the feelings or the actions of his characters: they speak and act, and, as in life, offer their utterance or their behavior as an outward clue to their inward secrets. In his painting of Gabrielle, Robinson is the true heir to the author of the *Scarlet Letter;* like Hawthorne, he searches the conscience, in the spirit of stern earnestness, which belongs to the puritan conception of the world. Gabrielle died of the conflict in her heart between passion and duty. The struggle is the more impressive as the moral force that compels her is not duty to her husband (who had neglected her), but duty to herself— awful reverence for the unwritten law. A coarser person might have lightly discarded what she would have considered as the shadowy impress of a distempered mood. She, under the stress of disquieting circumstances and with that morbid tendency which is wont to crop up in New England brains at a dire hour, follows the old puritan bias to self-harrowing and self-infliction. In this Robinson represents one side of the American mind, divided between the two extremes of buoyant energy and gnawing introspection. The latter is less frequent but more fraught with dramatic possibilities. It grows where a fatal heredity or long suffering have thinned and weakened the sources of life.

Robinson is not a contemner of the forces of life. Among the wrangling elements that tear fine-fibred souls, he may lean towards those that, through struggle and trial, make for love and joy, as in *The Book of Annandale.* Nothing is more conformable to the latest findings of the psychology of the subconscious than the inner struggle that dimly makes itself felt in the heart of Annandale on the day when his young wife was

214

buried. Nothing more arresting, because of its poignant realism, its dramatic impact, and the mysterious
aura that floats about it. After the cruel ceremonies of
the shrouding, the burial, and the parting with friends
and relatives, there comes to the bereaved young man
an uncalled-for moment of relief, such as an exhausted
frame will yield to, out of sheer incapacity to bear more.
Taking advantage of this surcease of sorrow, a feeling
creeps up in him from the depths, entirely foreign to
the situation and to his mood, hazy but insistent, unrecognized yet not to be resisted. The analysis of this
irresistible urge is conducted with as much surety as
delicacy. It brings with it an inexplicable mental hebe-
tude which makes Annandale angry with himself:

> He kept on wondering
> That he should feel so desolately strange
> And yet—for all he knew that he had lost
> More of the world than most men ever win—
> So curiously calm. . . . He could sigh,
> And he could even groan,—but what of that?
> There was no grief left in him. Was he glad?
> Yet how could he be glad, or reconciled,
> Or anything but wretched and undone?

In this bewildering state of feeling, he is haunted by
the thought of the beautiful female character, symbolic
of the poetry and force of love, which he has depicted in
a book written years before. Very aptly does this fascinating shape of ideal beauty impose itself on his vision,
for it is the embodiment of life, whispering its inevitable

215

appeal, even when it seems that despondency and death hold him under their sway.

We surmise that later—perhaps not so very much later—the coming of another woman will take him off his guard, breaking the last defence of his conscious self, loosing the forces that are clamoring for release. Then we are introduced to the other character of the story. In her case, we witness no unequal struggle between wavering reason and insidious impulse. Two feelings are equally strong in her and on a par, shaking her woman's frame to its foundation. Her old love has crystallized in the oath she took at her husband's death-bed; it raises in her pangs of conscience at the thought of possible desertion and perjury. Her womanly fidelity to her first maidenly attachment, her womanly sense of righteous doing, her womanly observance of the formulated rules of conduct, her womanly imagination, make her miserable when another feeling, opposed to the first, as strong as the first, begins to dawn in her consciousness. The poet's analysis vividly retraces her hesitations, her racking doubts, her self-arraignment, her incipient faint yielding to the fresh call of life, her recoil from the thought, finally the growing persuasion that she has suffered enough and that her husband himself would relieve her from the pledge.

Her path at last meets the path of Annandale and Life opens to them a vista of multiplied experience, with the warmth of love to their hearts and the radiancy of joy about their brows. The future is so bright for the very reason that they have sustained a hard debate with their conscience. They taught themselves and they taught each other; each, with the help of the other, became more worthy of sharing in the triumph of Life; each respected the other the more for pausing on the way. Such poetry, replete with truths of permanent and universal import, and, besides, creating beauty and emotion, is secure against waning or decay. Under a modern garb, it bears the classic quality that endures.

Annandale is a poet; but it is as a man, experiencing the vicissitudes of sorrow and of love, that we get interested in him. Robinson, in another production of his, tackles the great subject of the psychology of genius. The poem entitled *The Man Who Died Twice* brings in the forms of intense cerebral and affective activity which can be observed in a character gifted at once (as happens) with creative power and strong instincts. Through constructive imagination and dramatic expression, it emphasizes exceptional traits of the human mind and deals poignantly with pathological manifestations of the higher faculties.

When we come across Fernando Nash, musician and composer, he is so far gone on the downward grade as to be reduced to beating the big drum in a Salvation Army band. How he came to this plight, after giving in his young manhood splendid promise of artistic achievement, is what we shall learn from the man himself, confessing his own sad story. The poem is both a study in the degradation of genius and a dramatic picture of the appalling phases through which a large mind, lack-

217

ing strength, passes, before it reaches the last stage of helplessness and despair.

Fernando was conscious of the signal gift which distinguished him from the common herd and felt urged by an inward force to bring it to fruition. But his artistic nature was as exceptional for its possibilities of evil as for its capacity for good. He was as apt to yield to the lure of intemperance and lust as to listen to the call of beauty. Lack of self-control was the dire ransom of his brilliant endowments. The analysis of the awful soul-conflict affords materials for a noble poem, which Robinson makes intensely dramatic by the masterly construction of the episodes—all dealing with mental facts and spiritual values—and the fecundity of his imagination, prompt to visualize ideas in the shape of symbols.

A vivid light is thrown over the nature of genius and the mystery of inspiration. The artist has the distinct feeling of the outwardness, and, often, alas! of the elusiveness of the creative influx. In the pathetic account Fernando gives of his wasted life, a phrase comes again and again like a dismal burden: "I had it once!" —which plainly refers to a sudden illumination from above. His regrets express themselves in the bitter complaint: "I could not wait"—meaning that he was unable to keep down the lower self until the vision should become clear and he could translate it into a musical design. His propensity to vulgar reveling, he calls his "devils," which he let too often grapple by the throat his "daemon," or his better self. Addressing himself, he exclaims:

Your daemon had a lenience then,
And you had not the protest of a soul
Between you and your right to stay alive;
All which was as it was. But it was so
No longer when you knew it was not so,
And that one day a bush might bloom with fire
At any trivial hour of inattention,
Whereafter your employment would have been
A toil of joy for immortality.

This "trivial hour of inattention" powerfully suggests the sudden and irresponsible irruption of genius into the mind, in the midst of the trifling business of life. But Fernando could not turn into account the fleeting moments of supreme revelation, because he had failed to train his will and discipline his instincts. The subconscious in him was attuned to the higher mysteries; but when it shot its evanescent gleam into clear consciousness, it was choked there in a tumult of inchoate thoughts or gross sensations. Fernando had drifted through the better part of his life, now the sport of low impulses, now the imperfect instrument of inspiration, wafted from the depths to the heights—where he could not stay—lamentably passive. This had been the bane of his life and the ruin of his genius. When dizzied by the fumes of liquor or shaken by the beats of fever, his brains were invaded by a rumbling of drums, that destroyed all attempt at seizing any melodic phrase. This barbarous rattling becomes the symbol of his exile from the precincts of art. It breaks out thunderingly whenever he dares approach with an impure mind the sacred fountain-spring of heavenly strains.

One night, a last orgy dealt him a stunning blow, which laid him down in bed for several days. In his unquiet, feverish sleep, he is visited by visions, one of which is a dreadful musical nightmare, the other a mocking realization of artistic achievement. The contrast of these two visions is the culminating beauty of the poem. It derives its arresting power from the wealth of invention, the vivid antithesis between grim humor and glorious pageantry, and the intellectual significance contained in the concrete imagery. It brings together fantastic imagination, grotesque beauty, thrilling pathos, haunting symbols and plastic splendor. Psychological poetry reaches here its apex of fullness, intellectual vigor and suggestive appeal. We feel in the clutch of a dramatic force, risen from the mysterious depths of the soul. I can only quote a few lines from the second vision:

> And still the music sounded, weird but firm,
> And the more fearful as it forged along
> To a dark and surging climax, which at length
> Broke horribly into coarse and unclean laughter
> That rose above a groaning of the damned;
> And through it all there were those drums of death. . . .

From dismay to tragic emotion, we follow the startling changes of the vision. A faery edifice grows into space, a temple to beauty and to music,

> uprising lightly out of chaos
> And out of all the silence under time . . .

220

A chorus of voices and of instruments breaks out under the dome, and one triumphant motive soars above the melodious waves—the theme of supreme beauty, which the composer had been vainly pursuing all those years, able only to catch a few broken snatches of it. He experiences the exalted joy of the great artist who sees his dim intuition materialize into clear conception and thinks himself possessed of the means to invest it in shapes of final fixity. He has heard the great symphony that he might have written, but he is never to write it. He is once more placed face to face with the hard fact of his unworthiness to gather the golden harvest. His genius once more proves impotent, for lack of all that gives an artist's mind sustained power and an artist's life moral dignity. Fernando's desperate resolve to enlist in the Salvation Army to flee, as he says, from the "drums of death" to the "drums of life," emphasizes with grim philosophical irony the pathos of his spiritual defeat. It adds a touch of American local coloring to a tragedy of universal import, which, modern as it is in its symbolism and imagery, recalls the Greek drama by its human quality and its force of catharsis. It unites antique elevation of purpose with the essential novelty of a psychological plot based upon the late discoveries of the science of the subconscious.

Criticism brought against Robinson because of the unusualness of the cases treated in his poems is not valid. They are so chosen as to conform to general truth, although presenting one aspect of the truth in salient isolation and with the intensity which suits dramatic composition. Sophocles when he took up incest as the subject of *Œdipus Rex;* Shakespeare, when he put on the stage the murderous rage of a jealous husband; Racine, when he dramatized the love-fury of Phaedra, dealt with exceptional passions, which yet are kindred to the feelings of the average men and women, in whom they excite ready and awful sympathy. Pathological psychology is, for the same reason, a legitimate subject of modern poetry, not only by introducing pathetic incidents, which in our latter-day civilization hardly bear the character of rarity, but also by bringing poetry within the pale of science, in an age when intellectual curiosity is rampant, and in a field where science deals with mysterious facts particularly suited to the imaginative needs of poetry. The poet, with his sympathetic insight into the secrets of the human soul, becomes the fellow-worker of the psychologist, applying his method of observation, experiment and inference. The difference is that the imaginative writer makes use of the resources of his art to produce emotion and wonder.

Robinson's power to produce wonder is one of his supreme gifts. It rests, in the first place, on his masterly handling of composition. He generally precipitates us *in medias res,* taking us unawares, creating astonishment, arousing curiosity, then gradually revealing the facts, the motives, the strange passions or distractions of the characters, resolving the state of suspense to throw us into fluttered anxiety, shorn of painful acuteness by the moral atmosphere spread about the catastrophe. Keen analysis of states of mind, subtle description of emotional phases, startling pictures of visionary scenes or weird hallucinations, let us into the anguish, precarious joy, foreboding fear or miserable delusion which whirl the brains of the heroes. There is hardly any plot. Material events are scattered negligently, as it were, along the margin of the stream of feelings, as landmarks to measure its progress and show its direction. The variations of the emotions and the fluctuations of the inner struggle are the only things that count, as the most significant in the eyes of intelligent onlookers, the most fraught with suggestive truth, the most pregnant with imaginative appeal and power of affective sympathy. Robinson has no partiality for the facile intricacies of a clever intrigue or the cheap pathos of a melodramatic conclusion. His episodes have the intellectual quality and eminent dignity of the essentially human. He stands at the very antipodes of the vulgar forms of art, which, with the growth of the sensational drama and of the moving-picture shows, threaten to deteriorate American taste.

Another feature of his work is the delicate and impressive halo of mystery he conjures up about his poems, by sheer insight into the inarticulate vibrations and silent throbbings of the subconscious, and by promptness to seize the full significance of involuntary gestures or face-expressions. He does not need to have phantoms walk the earth or corpses rise from their bier, to make us feel the presence of the spiritual world. Without the paraphernalia of infernal pageantry, he can produce effects of ghostly shudder by his masterly handling of the eery deportment of distracted minds. He does not deal in horror, but rouses in us a sense of awe. His characters impress us by a strange flame in their eyes, unnatural silences broken by sudden outbursts of loquacity, superhuman self-possession exploding into violent fits of excitement, courteous behavior rent apart by flashes of flaming sarcasm, fixed ideas or haunting visions settling on the brain, stark callousness to ordinary feelings co-existing with passionate response to unreal constructions of the mind, and such-like tokens of mental derangement, obeying the abnormal logic of an intellect astray.

The mental sufferings of his heroes are true to nature, although in the routine of ordinary experience they do not reach such racking intensity. Over Norcross hovers the poisonous blight of a baneful heredity—the terrible legacy, at the hands of his New England ancestors (whose portraits hang on the walls of his home), of a nervous nature exhausted by two centuries of morbid self-searching and self-constraint. Avon is a broken-down business-man, who ruined his constitution (perhaps predestined to collapse) by hurried days and sleepless nights, and was whittled away to a mere shadow of himself, an intellectual wreck, a prey to gnawing fancies. Both are victims to the disintegrating forces that exert themselves in American civilization—and are not unknown in XXth century Europe. They may be too dismally true to win the assent of sentimental readers: but there is no denying their vividness, dramatic grandeur and weird reality.

In the handling of such fluid materials and subtle

values, much depends on the form. Let us, to conclude, cast a glance at the power of expression which accompanies the power to search the recesses of the human soul. Granting that Robinson's style may be at
times abstruse, overloaded with sense and sometimes too
intricate in period-building, it generally deserves high
praise for its propriety and precision, its chastened elegance in the intellectual passages and its magnificence
in imaginative description. While the richness of his
symbols and the splendor of his visions are often unequalled, he is no less a master of the direct, stripped
style, whose excellence lies in the perfect correspondence
of the words to the thought in the exact expression of
the shades of meaning, and in the sober coloring. What
galaxy of scintillating words could improve the simple
beauty of a passage like the following:

> So, for a year, it went . . . when, all at once,
> At someone's tinkling afternoon at home,
> I saw that in the eyes of Avon's wife
> The fire that I had met the day before
> In his had found another living fuel.
> To look at her and then to think of him,
> And thereupon to contemplate the fall
> Of a dim curtain over the dark end
> Of a dark play, required of me no more
> Clairvoyance than a man who cannot swim
> Will exercise in seeing that his friend
> Off shore will drown, except he save himself.

Robinson can intersperse his narratives with reflections of philosophical import, closely connected with
the analysis of the feelings and the dramatic movement

of the story, while bearing the mark of his magic manner of expression.   I quote from *Avon's Harvest*:

> Whether it was an evil chance alone,
> Or some invidious juggling of the stars,
> Or some accrued arrears of ancestors
> Who throve on debts that I was here to pay,
> Or sins within me that I knew not of,
> Or just a foretaste of what waits in hell
> For those of us who cannot love a worm,—
> Whatever it was, or whence or why it was,
> One day there came a stranger to the school . . .
> . . . his malignant oily swarthiness
> Housing a reptile blood—

Or we find an idea enshrined in a simile, which adds
an iridescence to its meaning, without detracting from
its stately dignity:

> A man who has no gold,
> Or an equivalent, shall pay no gold
> Until by chance or labor or contrivance
> He makes it his to pay; and he that has
> No kindlier commodity than hate,
> Glossed with a pity that belies itself
> In its negation, . . .
> What coin of God has he to pay the toll
> To peace on earth?

Thus, psychological notations take on a concrete fullness and a sensuous sheen, that give them power to
carry their impact beyond the intellect onto the
imagination and the heart.   A poet who can, with

thoughtful ease, run such a varied gamut of expression, still remaining himself, yet passing from bold flights of fancy and sumptuous descriptions to dense simplicity and restrained strength, is a great stylist. The outward beauty of Robinson's verse, gracefully and unerringly, in the best passages, moulds itself on his inspiration. His inspiration is distinguished by its depth and its intensity; his form not unseldom reaches sustained power and finality.

LAST WORD

THE co-existence in Robinson's poetical genius of the power of imaginative creation with the qualities of constructive thought, analytic scrutiny, strict decorum and just poise, is one of the reasons why I feel entitled to call him a modern classic. A century of multiplied and fecund attempts to renew and enrich the externals of poetry could not be lost for an artist so receptive of sensuous as well as ideal beauty, and so alive to the subtle kinship that binds the forms of nature to human thoughts and feelings. Robinson's faculty of translating intellectual and emotional values into visions, that, plain or gorgeous, enchant or thrill by their irresistible witchery, is closely related to the sensibility and imagination of a Wordsworth, a Coleridge, a Keats, a Browning, although he never borrows, but invents, with great felicity and fertility, on parallel lines with the admired founders of modern English poetry. The heir of the romanticists by his keen perception of all that the conquest of the realm of the senses and of the emotions has done for the enrichment of poetry, the precursor of the imagists by the concrete relief and glow of his painted scenes and their symbolic import, he resolutely leans towards the directness, simplicity, sanity and order, which in his mind are the only forms suited to a sincere observation of facts, a clear-sighted understanding of character, a balanced interpretation of conduct and a vigorous insight into the permanent truths of life. That classic bias and that method of equable composition and rational development have led some critics to overlook the breadth and variety of inspiration which find free play in his mind. A hasty survey of his production may indeed leave a false impression, if one mistakes for sameness or monotony the intellectual and artistic unity produced by the constant presence of reasonableness and restraint. I do not contend that there is no trace of mannerism in his work. But an attentive and sympathetic study reveals a wide field of interests and a rich palette of shadings, where delicacy and power blend in ripe harmony. We live in the age of the eccentric, the brawling, the morbid—or at least the experimental. The feverishness of our civilization, the loudness of much of what passes for literature, the incessant change and whirl in the business-world as well as in the world of art, make it difficult for our contemporaries to appreciate a style of poetry which clothes its strength and glow in sober raiment and modestly keeps away from the spot-light, shy to advertise itself.

It requires steadiness, patience, continuity of purpose and a certain willingness and pliancy to become a familiar of Robinson's poetry and open oneself to its influence. The readers who make the preliminary effort of initiation will not waste their pains. They will discover much more than any formal analysis can suggest, for they will find themselves in contact with a deep nature and an original genius, whose quiet ways hide abundant reserves of rich humanity.